HOMEMADE
Cream Liqueurs

HOMEMADE
Cream Liqueurs

DONA AND MEL MEILACH

CONTEMPORARY
BOOKS, INC.
CHICAGO ▪ NEW YORK

Library of Congress Cataloging-in-Publication Data

Meilach, Dona.
Homemade cream liqueurs.

Includes index.
1. Meilach, Mel.   2. Liqueurs—Amateurs' manuals.   I. Title.
TP611.M438   1986   641.2'55   85-28997
ISBN 0-8092-5121-3

Copyright © 1986 by Dona Meilach and Mel Meilach
All rights reserved
Published by Contemporary Books, Inc.
180 North Michigan Avenue, Chicago, Illinois 60601
Manufactured in the United States of America
Library of Congress Catalog Card Number: 85-28997
International Standard Book Number: 0-8092-5121-3

Published simultaneously in Canada by Beaverbooks, Ltd.
195 Allstate Parkway, Valleywood Business Park
Markham, Ontario L3R 4T8 Canada

To Jordan, Adam, and Zachary Seligman

Contents

Acknowledgments

Preparing this book was made much easier, thanks to the help of Heublein, Inc. and Hiram Walker, Inc. These companies provided samples, clear liqueurs for mixing and testing, and permission to alter and incorporate recipes developed in their kitchens.

Our thanks to our neighbors and friends, Pat Hoines and Evelyn Camp, for letting us borrow china, glass, linen, and artifacts for the assorted props used in styling and photographs.

Our appreciation to Patrick Worley, president of The Plant Kingdom, Lincoln Acres, California, for the sensitive drawings. As the floral artist for his company's catalog, he was happy to transfer his talents to another subject.

To our unsuspecting friends, who became enthusiastic tasters at dinner parties, we were delighted with your positive reactions. Those of you who "dropped by" at other times to see what our refrigerator and freezer yielded, we want you to know we love the bond that good food and friendship fosters.

To our editor, Nancy Crossman, who originated the idea, our gratitude for suggesting this follow-up to our successful earlier book *Homemade Liqueurs*.

Dona and Mel Meilach
Rancho, LaCosta, Carlsbad, California

1 What's in a Cream Liqueur?

Do you have a sweet tooth that relentlessly craves some new confection? A different taste treat? One that thrives on smooth, creamy concoctions? Then you're a candidate for cream liqueurs—the latest, luscious entry into the liquor market.

Lest you confuse the new "cream" liqueurs with the familiar clear liqueurs or with those with the words "crème de" before them, now is the time to define each type and establish firmly which are which.

Cream liqueurs (the new drinks on the market) have real cream added. Their taste resembles a liquor-flavored milk shake. They have an opaque, milky appearance and a consistency similar to a thin milk shake. The ingredients are blended, unlike those of clear liqueurs, which are steeped. Cream liqueurs are ready to drink after blending.

A *clear* liqueur (non-cream) has a waterlike consistency. It may have no color, or it may be amber, cherry-red, or blue from berries, depending on the color inherent in the flavoring or fresh fruit used in the steeping process. This process is also called "macerating" and is similar to steeping tea. Flavors are added to vodka or brandy, which is then sweetened and aged.

Making both cream and clear liqueurs is easier, faster, and yields more immediate results than making wine or other alcoholic liquids that must be fermented or distilled. Of the two, cream liqueurs take less time to make than clear liqueurs and are ready for drinking when they come out of the blender.

Creating a cream liqueur is fun. You probably can begin now with products you have on your shelf and in the refrigerator. It could become:

- a hobby yielding new taste treats,
- an adventure in dining and drinking,
- a fresh approach for cooking and baking,
- a sophisticated addition to all your entertaining.

Cream liqueur making can put you steps ahead of anyone else—and only you will know how much pleasure and how little expense and effort are involved.

SORTING OUT THE LIQUEUR TYPES

You probably are aware of clear liqueurs such as Amaretto, Kahlùa, Frangelico, Tia Maria, Drambuie, Grand Marnier, Sabra, and scores of other well-known flavors and brands that use vodka or brandy as a base.

Next are those with a *crème de* in front of the flavor name: crème de menthe, crème de cacao, etc. They are similar to the clear liqueurs, but are sweeter.

Liqueurs that have the word *cream* following the name make up another category. A flavor is mixed with a spirit such as Irish whiskey, cognac, bourbon, gin, rum, vodka—or a combination of spirits. Then, rich dairy cream is added. Among popular flavors and brands advertised are: Chocolate Cream, American Cream, Irish Cream, Amaretto Cream, Häagen-Dazs Cream, and others.

What are the characteristics of a cream liqueur? A smooth, creamy, dreamy drink that could be compared to a freshly frothed milk shake with a kick of liquor for a wicked taste experience. Or compare it to a rich, softened ice cream laced with rum or another sinfully delicious flavor.

Probably the cream drink you've heard of, or seen advertised most, is Baileys Original Irish Cream Liqueur. Baileys was the originator of this spirited genre of genius that pumped generous globs of gold into the company that made and distributed it beginning in 1979. Baileys also fostered a variety of imitators and competitors who picked up the cue and developed similar and additional flavors.

Companies that jumped into the cream liquor market keep their formulas and techniques so close to the chest that no one is allowed a peek into their "proprietary" methods and recipes. The whole industry seems to have taken an oath to never, never reveal any of its secrets to *anyone*.

What are *cordials*? That's another word for *liqueurs*; the two are used interchangeably.

Ratafia is also synonymous with liqueur and cordial.

Eau de vie is a generic term for spirits made of fruits and alcohol that have been distilled with no added sweetener.

WHY MAKE CREAM LIQUEURS YOURSELF?

Give us something we are told we can't copy and we'll try to come close. It's not possible to duplicate the elixirs made by industry; a home kitchen lacks the controls, the mechanical mixing methods, and the straight-from-the-cow-at-the-right-season creams. However it is possible to create a blend that looks and tastes similar to the purchased concoctions—and that's the challenge.

But challenge is only one reason for making cream liqueurs yourself. Another reason is to create new recipes—and new ways to use them. That's the premise of this book.

Some people thrive on tackling new recipes: they have a flair for experimentation, a penchant for creativity, an urge to add a little of this and that. They are like mad magicians and their results are more original than rabbits pulled out of hats.

For those who prefer to follow where others have led, you'll discover ample recipes and ideas for concocting a variety of individual tasting cream liqueurs. These are followed by scores of recipes using the cream liqueurs you make. You'll learn how to add these liqueurs to recipes you already use. You may never again be happy with plain cheesecake after you've made one with Irish double-chocolate cream liqueur.

Need another reason to embark on this easy journey to discovery? You'll save money. A fifth of cream liqueur from your local liquor store varies, depending on brand name and accompanying advertising budget, from about seven to eighteen dollars at this writing. Making the same or greater quantities as contained in a commercial bottle will cost you less than half. Or, put another way, if you spend the same amount of money on ingredients that a commercial fifth costs, you'll generate more than twice the amount. And there are no import taxes to pay.

Another economy? Buy a fifth of commercial liqueur and you'll have to drink it up in a few weeks or the taste may change. Make your liqueurs in small batches and they won't last long. You can try a new flavor quickly. If you don't like it, you haven't lost much.

Making cream liqueurs can be faster than running to the store to buy them. Suppose you have unexpected guests coming in an hour? You can whip up a favorite batch just before they arrive and it's ready to serve on the rocks or in a delicately stemmed liqueur glass.

You can safely bet on another bonus. When you serve homemade liqueurs to your friends for dessert or after dinner you can provide them with a variety of flavors that does not exist elsewhere. Serve them for sipping or sauces, in drinks or desserts. You can become the host or hostess known for heady, hearty happenings. And that's only the tip of the ice cube.

You can use all pure, fresh ingredients—no artificial emulsifiers, no preservatives. Read the labels on some commercial products and discover how loaded they are with preservatives and artificial flavorings. When you make the liqueurs yourself everything can be fresh. The result may be a different taste— a difference that often makes them better.

WHO DRINKS CREAM LIQUEURS?

When cream liqueurs were first popular, according to liquor store owners, men thought that it wasn't "macho" to drink them. Cream liqueurs were "sissy," a drink for women who loved their mildness and sweet taste. With an alcohol content lower than hard liquor, small servings could be handled easily by social drinkers.

However, men soon learned that behind these soothing, sweet drinks were tastes that could not be overlooked. Soon they, too, were buying the bottles for their bars and imbibing as enthusiastically as their wives and girlfriends.

It wasn't long before commercials appeared that were designed to entice everyone to enjoy the goodness of creamy liqueurs. Sales shot up, new brands and flavors appeared on shelves, and bartenders created new drinks.

And now we've created the recipes for you to use to make cream liqueurs yourself and then incorporate them into drinks, cakes, pies, cookies, candies, and a variety of other goodies.

CREAM LIQUEURS ARE GREAT FOR GIFTS

Keep ingredients, a few fancy bottles, and labels on hand, and you can whip up a batch of cream liqueurs for gifts at your next dinner party. Make them for Christmas presents, or as a surprise-something-to-take-home-to-remember item when people come to your house.

HOW DO YOU KNOW WHAT MAKES
A GOOD CREAM LIQUEUR?

We provide recipes that we have tried and combinations we have concocted, but the possibilities are infinite. Just as companies, each year, introduce new flavors and blends after experimentation and taste testing, you can do the same—only you don't have to wait a year. You don't have at stake a million dollars worth of research and development and an advertising campaign. Use your imagination, the ingredients on hand, and your own taste buds to provide answers. Dare to be inventive—the worst that will happen is that you may waste a little liquor and cream (although you'll probably consume it during the testing process).

For flavor ideas, study labels on bottles of commercial varieties and taste test them by buying large bottles or miniatures. You can also taste test at a restaurant or bar, or when you see a bottle at someone else's house.

As you study labels, you'll note that some varieties are made with "non-dairy cream." Observe that these are *not* called "cream liqueurs" on the label. (Laws prevent using the word *cream* unless real cream is in the product). They have the spelling "crème" or "crema" in the name (as opposed to liqueurs that are "crème de"). The non-dairy crème liqueurs predated fresh cream liqueurs, but many of the former are still popular. Examples are Piña Colada Crème, Quincy Market Toasted Almond Crème, Amaretto Crème Liquore, and the "black cow" type drinks. Their labels will inspire flavor combinations you can create with fresh creams. We do not include recipes for using artificial cream in this book, but you might want to try them on your own.

SOME POPULAR CREAM LIQUEURS

VARIETY	ORIGIN	FLAVOR	SPIRIT
American Creme	United States	mocha caramel	brandy
Baileys Original Irish Cream	Ireland	rich dairy cream	Irish whiskey
Carolans	Ireland	dairy cream, honey	Irish whiskey
Conticream	Australia	coffee, chocolate	Scotch
Cremaretto	Italy	chocolate, cream	amaretto
Emmets	Ireland	chocolate, natural flavors	brandy
Creme de Grand Marnier Liqueur	France	orange	brandy
Haagen-Dazs	United States	various flavors	French Cognac
Leroux	Ireland	natural flavors, dairy cream	Irish whiskey
Myers's Original Rum Cream	Jamaica	dairy cream	rum
Original Cream	United States	coffee, other flavors	Scotch
O'Darby	Ireland	chocolate, other flavors	whiskey
Piña Colada Liqueur	Jamaica	pineapple, coconut	rum
Venetian Cream	Italy	natural flavors, dairy cream	brandy
Waterford Cream	Ireland	chocolate, vanilla	Irish whiskey
Wimbledon	United States	strawberries	neutral base
VOV	Italy	eggnog, like zabaglione	Marsala wine

HOW DID CREAM
LIQUEURS COME TO BE?

Baileys Original Irish Cream was the first of the fresh cream liqueurs as we know them today. When it was imported and introduced by The Paddington Corporation in September 1979, as Baileys Irish Cream, it was an instant hit. Since that time, a variety of different flavors and spirit combinations have hit the market each year, which caused Paddington to add the word "Original" to the Baileys name.

There were a few precursors to the product. A brand called "Greensleeves" was test marketed in Chicago in mid-1979, but it never took off. A few years earlier, a series of "Hereford Cow" cream liqueurs, made with an artificial cream formula, had appeared. There were problems: the cream separated from the spirit so the shelf life was short and impractical for mass marketing.

R. & A. Bailey & Company, Ltd., of Dublin, Ireland, discovered the formula for stabilizing cream and alcohol in 1975, but the company kept it highly secret. It was essential that the natural cream base be stabilized so it would not separate from the Irish whiskey base. Part of the formula required that the proof (alcoholic strength) be exactly thirty-four; higher or lower would nullify the liquid's stability. With the formula perfected, the Bailey Company worked at developing a marketable product and amassing necessary market research. The company also needed to be sure the formula would sustain a twelve- to eighteen-month shelf life.

Market research in 1977 revealed that people liked the taste of a cream liqueur; it was entirely new, and the cream cut the harshness of the whiskey flavor. Women said, "Cream makes whiskey taste good." That supported research that has indicated that Americans really don't like the taste of alcohol.

Once Baileys Irish Cream was launched, the company's major problem was trying to supply enough for the demand. Why? The production of the liqueur depended on nature—the ability of cows to produce milk. Normally, that would be no problem, but the Baileys formula required a high pH cream to guarantee stability. The metabolism of cows changes during the month of March; the cream they produce has a higher acid content (lower pH). The demand for producing cream liqueurs at that time is high (it's a popular summertime drink), but production has to be cut back while awaiting the cream with a lower acid content. Cream that is too high in acetic must be rejected and there is inordinate waste. This helps account for Baileys' high price.

By April 1980, American companies also uncovered the secret to the natural-cream and whiskey stability. The American company, Emmets, had a competitive edge. Emmets was already in the dairy business, so their dairy technology was more advanced than that of the European-based Baileys. Emmets had other outlets for cream that couldn't be used in liqueurs; it could be made into cheeses and other milk products so no waste was incurred. The product, however, was, and still is, created in Ireland in the "dairylands of County Caven from the purest of rich Irish Cream laced with the finest spirits and flavors" according to the label. (It is imported by "21" Brands, Inc., New York.)

Improvements in technology permitted Emmets to eliminate one step in the manufacture of Emmets "Ireland's Cream Liqueur." That factor, combined with no waste, resulted in a product that could sell for less than Baileys.

Emmets had another ingredient: smart marketing. The Emmets managers ruled out an investment for heavy advertising. The product was designated as a *store owners' brand*, which meant that when a customer balked at the fourteen-dollar price of Baileys, the dealer could offer an alternate brand of equal quality at approximately five dollars less. The store would not lose the sale, and the customer would generally become a repeat buyer of the lower-priced label.

Today at least thirty-seven brands are on the market, each with a varying spirit base and combination of flavorings. Some companies list the ingredients on the bottle but, of course, not the formula, which is always considered "proprietary."

LIQUEURS BEFORE CREAMS EVOLVED

What led up to cream liqueurs? Clear liqueurs have been around since the thirteenth century, when they were invented by monks who were seeking a cure for stomach distress. Historians note that Hippocrates in the fifth century B.C. is believed to have been the first man to flavor alcohol with herbs and aromatic plants, but his brew is described as "fit only for the strongest men."

The monks were the ones who, working in the monasteries during the Middle Ages, did research in mixing spices and fruits with the distilled spirits they discovered. Their original blends were believed to be harsh and almost as hard to take as the stomach distress they were designed to cure. Christopher Columbus had a role in this history; he brought sugarcane from the New World. When sweetener was added to the stomach elixirs, the earliest varieties of the liqueurs that we know today were born.

Probably the oldest and best known liqueur is Benedictine, first produced in the monastery of the Benedictine monks at Fécamp Abbey, France. The original Benedictine recipe contains twenty-seven different herbs and dried plants, including Ceylon tea, juniper berries, balm, angelica, cinnamon, cloves, nutmeg, vanilla, and more. The Benedictine available in our stores today is based on that same original recipe.

Many liqueur producing monasteries are still open to the public. In Italy, near Florence, one can fan out in various directions and find them. They all maintain *pharmacias*, or bars, where small bottles of their blends may be tasted and purchased at a nominal cost. Alas, the history of cream liqueurs is short and not nearly so romantic as clear liqueurs. Cream liqueurs were produced to be a commercial success in a competitive market.

HOW AND WHEN TO SERVE LIQUEURS

Certain drinks used to be served in special glasses. Clear liqueurs were traditionally served in stemmed glasses with tiny bowls from which one would sip the drink slowly and delicately, and which would simultaneously direct the aroma to the nostrils. These liqueurs were also thought to be only an "after-dinner drink."

Erase those images from your mind! You can serve liqueurs in any kind of glass you like, by themselves, or mixed with other spirits. (See Chapter 4.)

When to drink them? The vice-president of a large company in the industry noted that drinking liqueurs "anytime" had to be stressed—"if all the after-dinner-only liqueur business went to only one producer, that firm would soon be out of business."

He reported that it is the consumers themselves who develop ideas that filter back to industry leaders. Consumers probe the potential versatility of the drinks, while marketing managers drag their feet.

HAVE A TASTE-TESTING PARTY

Part of the fun of creating liqueurs is showing off newfound formulas and sharing them with others. The ultimate treat to try at parties is to have your friends taste test the liqueurs and to let them guess what you put into the dessert you served.

We stumbled on the idea of tasting and guessing out of necessity. Our struggle to find the right combinations and methods made us biased toward our drink replicas. No, not replicas, for we were sure we had surpassed the commercial varieties in taste. We were convinced ours were better. But were they?

We tossed a dinner party and invited our unsuspecting friends. We trotted out our blind-labeled bottles of assorted sizes and shapes, each designated by number, some containing commercial liqueurs and others containing our homemade liqueurs. Our guests poured, dipped, and sipped, using ladles and spoons and 1-ounce disposable plastic glasses.

No one could discern which were the commercial varieties. Generally, the commercial flavors were deemed "less pronounced in taste" than ours. Our more exotic flavors were favored: blueberry and orange creams topped the list, even among chocoholics who, we thought, would vote for the double chocolate chip. "But chocolate is chocolate," said one person. "Orange and blueberry cream? They are quite different."

Nothing was left at the end of the evening. We made additional batches to corroborate our guests' votes by trying them on anyone who chanced to cross our kitchen threshold.

The conclusion? The combinations are so good, you can't go far wrong with anything you make. So read on, gather your ingredients, and get a quick education in liqueur making. It could be the easiest master's degree you'll ever earn.

2 *Beginning with the Basics*

Mixing cream liqueurs is as easy as making a milk shake. Your options for taste treats are greater because spirits are added. The beauty of it is that there are no distilling or fermenting processes to master and none of the aging and waiting time that other liquors need. And it's legal! Just combine the ingredients in your blender, pour, and enjoy.

You can emulate the taste, consistency, and color of commercial cream liqueur varieties, but you can't duplicate them. And you may not want to; the ability to alter flavors and experiment with taste combinations is a big plus.

You write all the rules for making liqueurs the way *you* like them. You can use basic raw ingredients: flavorings, spirits, milk, and eggs. Another approach is to begin with clear commercial liqueurs or homemade liqueurs to which you can add cream and other spirits. Sometimes you'll feel like a kitchen wizard concocting a magic brew.

A few problems exist that are easily overcome. You can't control the amount of acidity or buttermilk content in the cream or the exact proof of your final product. Nor do you have the advantage of mechanical homogenization. Flavorings and the quality of fresh ingredients vary. You won't be able to stabilize the mixes and provide as long a storage life as their commercial counterparts. The alcohol base you use may affect the taste.

Therefore, when you try to simulate an Irish cream liqueur, you are making your own version. You can't duplicate a Baileys or an Emmets brand (that would be illegal). Your result will be your unique brand; you might want to label it as such.

Almost every combination we tried was delicious, even when it didn't taste like the liqueurs we bought for making taste comparisons. When a result was too sweet we adjusted the ingredients the next time around. If the spirit base was too strong or harsh, we substituted another, or combined the stronger spirit with a smoother one. The experimenting, wondering, and tasting were part of the excitement.

SEPARATION AND THICKENING

You should have little trouble with ingredients separating from each other if you follow the directions for blending (pages 23–24). It is important to add ingredients in the given order and to use our blending methods. If the ingredients separate when you are experimenting with your own combinations, add one or two eggs to the mix. Always shake or stir liqueurs before using, whether they are homemade or commercial.

Homemade mixtures made with fresh fruits may tend to thicken as they stand because the fruits contain natural pectin, a thickening agent. We recommend using low butterfat milk with fresh fruit—mixing the milk into the fruit and spirit at low speed only long enough to blend. Do not overmix; when air is incorporated into the mixture, it will thicken.

If the liqueurs you make are not as stable as the commercial varieties, there is an answer. Mix small batches and use them quickly. We recommend keeping a batch for no longer than four to six weeks.

SHELF LIFE

Homemade liqueurs have a shorter shelf life than commercially made products because the homemade mixtures lack stabilizers and are not produced under laboratory-controlled conditions. Despite the preservative quality of the spirits, flavors tend to change over time. But that's true of commercial products, too.

Commercially made cream liqueurs have a shelf life, unopened, of twelve to eighteen months. Why this great time variation? It depends on the conditions under which a liqueur is stored. You'll observe that all cream liqueurs are in brown bottles; this is done to reduce the amount of light that reaches the contents.

Heat and light are the enemies of cream liqueurs. In warm climates unopened bottles should be stored in cool rooms, never near windows. When cream liqueurs are displayed in store windows in warm weather, the temperatures could easily exceed 110° F. At those temperatures, the liquid will break up and visibly separate. The condition is irreversible. Shaking the bottle will appear to remix the contents, but the remixing will be temporary and the taste will be affected.

After a bottle of commercial cream liqueur is opened it should be consumed promptly or refrigerated, especially in warm weather.

FREEZING—SUCCESSFUL AND RECOMMENDED

As we experimented with the recipes for this book, we often created more cream liqueur than we could consume or use in baking. Because of short shelf life and lack of refrigerator space, we resorted to freezing small quantities, about ¾ to 1 cup, in sterilized jelly jars.

We took the frozen liqueurs out a jar at a time as needed for testing, drink mixing, and adding to baked goods. We felt there was little or no appreciable taste or texture difference from refrigerated liqueurs. We froze some of the liqueurs from four to six months and were pleased with their taste at the end of the time periods. But once rerefrigerated, some seemed to get stronger after a few days. That demonstrates the wisdom of freezing them in small-sized jars.

We also froze commercial cream liqueurs. They too seemed about the same after freezing as when the bottle was first opened. When we asked marketing managers of liqueur companies how *they* felt about freezing their product, none could comment because they had no experience with the concept. That's understandable. From a marketing viewpoint, why recommend it? The object is to drink the product quickly during its short shelf life, then buy more.

EQUIPMENT NEEDED

To make cream liqueurs from scratch, you need a blender, measuring cups and spoons, and a can opener. A wire whisk is a worthwhile addition.

To make a flavored clear liqueur as a base for a cream liqueur, you will need additional supplies. This equipment is discussed in the section that explains how to make clear liqueurs (pages 31–32).

Bottles and Bottling

You may have observed that commercial cream liqueurs are always marketed in brown bottles. The object is to protect the milk; light tends to accelerate spoiling. However, even dark bottles cannot protect the contents from heat. When exposed to heat the solutions may separate and even the taste of commercial products may be severely altered. When a commercial cream liqueur spoils, some ingredients thicken, rise to the top, and plug the neck of the bottle. When a liqueur will not pour, chances are it is spoiled.

You can recycle commercial liqueur bottles for home use. Make sure they are sterilized by washing them in a dishwasher or boiling them, as for canning.

When brown bottles are not available, don't fret. We have used clear bottles without travail. Because they are refrigerated, they are in a dark environment. You may wrap the bottles with brown paper and a rubber band, if you like, to prevent light from hitting them when the refrigerator door is opened.

We haven't worried about the brown bottle situation for another reason: we drink the mixtures before a microbe could think of multiplying. When we know we won't use the liqueurs quickly, they go into small bottles in the freezer.

The narrow neck of a recycled commercial liqueur bottle can pose problems if the elixir you make thickens. It is easier to pour from a corked or screw-covered, wide-mouth jar. When we know the mix is of pouring consistency, we move it to another, fancier jar if we plan to serve the liqueur to company.

For small quantities, sterilized, recycled jelly jars work well. Watch for dark bottles in antique shops. Those that are well-designed are perfect for gift giving.

Labels, Notes, and Record Keeping

Label each jar carefully and keep a log of what you have mixed for future reference. Record any ingredients added or subtracted from the basic recipe and how you changed it. You may wish to make a recipe and then divide it in half, trying some flavorings in one half and different flavors or spirits in the other half.

RECIPE RECORD

The record might consist of:

Recipe name _____

Date made _____

Half or full recipe

Ingredients *(in order added and amount)*

____   _____

____   _____

____   _____

____   _____

____   _____

____   _____

Length of blending time and speed used _____

Number of cups yielded _____

Consistency at time mixed _____

Consistency after storage: one day   _____

one week   _____

two weeks   _____

Comments _____

Taste _____

Next time try _____

_____

THREE WAYS TO CREATE CREAM LIQUEURS

In Chapter 1, we explained the difference between cream and clear liqueurs. Now, we will consider three categories of cream liqueurs based on how they are created: those made from scratch, those made from commercial clear liqueurs, and those which use homemade clear liqueurs as a base.

Making Cream Liqueurs from Scratch

The commercial brands that you will initially try to emulate are: Baileys Original Irish Cream, Häagen-Dazs, American Cream, Emmets, and so on. Then you'll go on to make your own flavors.

When cream liqueurs are made from scratch, the ingredients are:

> flavorings—various coffees, vanilla, chocolate, coconut, mint, nuts, and fresh fruits
> whiskey blends, scotch, bourbon, brandy, cognac, vodka, rum, etc.
> canned or fresh cream and/or milk
> eggs (in some recipes)

Advantages: Your creativity and invention in combining flavorings and spirit bases. Fast, easy. Less expensive than commercial varieties. More fun to make when you do it all yourself. When results are delicious, you'll enjoy the compliments. Ingredients are readily available and can be stored on kitchen shelf. You can use all fresh ingredients—no preservatives. You can control the richness by eliminating or reducing the egg and control the sweetness by using more evaporated milk and less sweetened condensed milk. You can reduce calories by using low-fat milks.

Disadvantages: Flavors may vary from batch to batch with quality of fruit. May combine flavors and spirits you don't like. May take some experimentation to achieve desired results.

Commercial cream liqueurs are almost always thirty-four or thirty-five proof, about seventeen percent alcohol by volume. The proof of homemade products will be more variable.

Making Cream Liqueurs from Commercial Clear Liqueurs

You can use familiar, off-the-shelf clear liqueurs as a flavor base. They include amaretto, Kahlùa, Grand Marnier, Sabra, schnapps, and many other varieties you're accustomed to seeing in ads, liquor stores, and bars.

These are made with:

> flavorings
> spirit, which is usually vodka or brandy

The proof is high and varies from about forty to as high as sixty. (Commercial liqueurs can be as much as one hundred proof.)

Crème de varieties such as crème de cacao, crème de menthe, and crème de banana are made in the same way as the above liqueurs but are sweeter because they contain twice as much sugar syrup. The proof is lower, generally in the thirty-five to fifty-five range.

Advantages: Fast, easy. Consistent flavor.

Disadvantages: Relatively expensive. Not so creative or experimental as liqueurs made from scratch.

Making Homemade Clear Liqueurs as a Base for Creams

Make the base clear liqueur by steeping the flavoring in vodka. Age. Sweeten. Then, use that liqueur in the same way as you would a commercial liqueur and add cream, milk, and egg.

Homemade clear liqueurs made without cream may be stored much longer than cream liqueurs, usually about eight months.

Advantages: Inexpensive. Can create infinite flavor variations and combinations. Liqueur flavorings, concentrates, and extracts are commercially available for ease and consistent taste.

Disadvantages: Making the base liqueur requires steeping time from a few days to three to four weeks before it is made into a cream liqueur. Most have a vodka or a brandy base. Flavors of fresh ingredients may vary with season. How long dried flavorings have been stored also can affect flavor.

COMPARING PROOFS IN COMMERCIAL LIQUEURS

Proof is the measure of the strength of the alcohol. One degree of proof equals one-half of one percent of alcohol. Think of the proof number as about double the percentage of alcohol by volume. Therefore, a bottle labeled one hundred proof is about fifty percent alcohol. Cream liqueurs at thirty-four proof contain about seventeen percent alcohol by volume. The percentage is not exact because of the effect that alcohol has on water when they are mixed. The proof is slightly more than double the percentage.

ALCOHOLIC CONTENT
OF COMMERCIAL LIQUEURS,
BY PROOF

Here are examples of the proof in some commercial liqueurs:

Liqueur	Degree of Proof
Amaretto	54–56°
Frangelico	56°
Grand Marnier	80°
Irish Mist	80°
Peppermint schnapps	100°
Crème de almond	54°
Crème de banana	54–56°
Crème de cacao	56°
American Cream	34°
Baileys Irish Cream	34°
Demi-Tasse	34°

THE BLENDING FACTOR—
ESSENTIAL PROCEDURES

Pay special attention to how you blend the ingredients. This factor can make the difference between the success and failure of the consistency of the cream liqueur. The goal is to minimize the amount of air you mix into the creams and, especially, the eggs. For this reason, a lidded blender or food processor used at low speed (rather than an open-top electric mixer bowl) is recommended.

Pulse Stir

Mix the flavor and spirit at a medium to high speed. Add the creams, blending at a low speed. Add eggs last (where called for) and use a *pulse* action on the *stir* or slowest setting your appliance has. *Pulse stir means you use an on-off procedure about eight times during one minute.*

Blending Ingredients in Order

The *order* in which you add ingredients makes a difference, too. Combine flavoring with the spirit and blend on medium or high settings about one minute. Then, add the canned or fresh creams or milks and blend at low speed for one minute. Always add the eggs last and stir for the shortest amount of time: about one minute at pulse stir. The entire blending procedure from beginning to end is a maximum of four minutes.

Remember you *do not* want cream or fresh cream products such as whipping cream or heavy cream and/or egg whites to thicken as you would when they are used in cakes. By adding them last and using pulse action, less air is incorporated. Or, they can be thoroughly stirred with a wire whisk, added to the flavoring/whiskey mixture, and then whisked until smooth.

Fresh ingredients such as peaches, berries, bananas, nuts, and so on, should be pureed in a blender and measured. The amount used should not make up more than one-fourth or one-fifth of the volume of the entire recipe. If too much of the fresh ingredient is used, the mixture may thicken; many fruits contain natural thickening agents. Use subtly flavored spirits or a mixture of spirit and vodka so the fruit flavor is not overpowered.

A thick, spoonable result should not be considered a failure. Use it for baking or for spooning over ice creams and cakes as a sauce. Experiment with thinning methods (pages 30–31).

When you add creams to clear liqueurs (as opposed to

making the liqueurs from scratch), combine the ingredients in the blender and mix as you would a milk shake, but *add any eggs last and pulse stir them.*

THE FLAVOR FACTOR

Cream liqueurs are in the infant stage of being marketed compared to clear liqueurs and liquors, so the flavors used have been limited. The commercial varieties are combinations of chocolate, coffee, vanilla, almond, or the "secret proprietary combinations." Some companies simply state on the label that "other natural flavors" are used.

Each season, and usually before Christmas when liqueur sales are at an apex, new flavors are added to stimulate buyers' palates and spending.

You can beat the commercial liqueur makers at their own game and use likely combinations based on your own preferences and what you have on your kitchen shelf and in your private bar.

We have added coconut, fresh fruits, herbs and spices, flavored extracts, fresh juices, and flavored coffees. You can add flavorings such as cinnamon, cloves, and nutmeg.

For extra zest, originality, and sensational taste, you can purposely leave particles of the flavoring ingredient suspended in the liquid. Examples are: tiny bits of chocolate chip and bits remaining from berries, peaches, and other fruits that do not break down when they are chopped in the blender.

THE SPIRIT FACTOR

The majority of clear liqueurs have vodka as their base because vodka has no inherent flavor. But cream liqueurs have different purposes and the flavor of the spirit combined with the flavorings and quality of the cream can add taste and texture.

Spirits vary because of their ingredients and the manner in which they are prepared. When you experiment, the combinations you could use are infinite. Baileys Original Irish Cream

Liqueur is made with Irish whiskey; American Cream Liqueur is made with an American whiskey; therein lies the difference. Häagen-Dazs is made with cognac, while McGuires Original Cream is scotch-based.

The differences among the major liquor (spirit) categories are described to help you decide which you may select, and eventually prefer.

Brandy

There are three classic types of brandy: cognac, Armagnac, and California. Cognac and Armagnac are named for the towns from which they originate in southwestern France. They are made from nondescript wines. California brandy obviously is named for the state in which it is produced.

Cognac has a complex distillation process. It is aged in oak from two to five years. When ready for bottling, it is diluted to a forty-proof alcohol. Then, caramel is added for color and some sugar is added for taste.

Armagnac is drier in flavor than cognac. The distillation process is less complex and no sugar is added.

California brandy is aged in special stills. Some caramel syrup is added for color and flavor.

Other brandies, generally less costly than the classic types, are made all over the world by varying methods with color, sugar, and flavoring materials added. Brandies generally are eighty to eighty-four proof.

Whiskey

Whiskey is made from grains such as corn, rye, barley, and wheat. The fermented mash of the grain is distilled and then aged in oak barrels. During aging, it attains its color, flavor, and aroma. Whiskies from different countries are distinct from one another because of the characteristics of the local grains used and the techniques, times, and formulas for distillation. That's why you will see whiskeys labeled Scotch, Irish,

American, Kentucky, Canadian, Australian, etc. Whiskeys generally are about eighty proof.

The United States—Over thirty-three distinct types of whiskey are produced in the United States; they are termed *American blended light whiskey*. Bourbon is the major American produced whiskey; it is distilled from a barley malt and ground corn and is aged more than four years in new (charred) oak barrels. Bourbon was originally named for Bourbon County in Kentucky where it originated. Today, Illinois, Indiana, Ohio, Pennsylvania, Tennessee, and Missouri also produce bourbon. Other American whiskeys are made from corn, rye, and various blends.

Ireland—Irish whiskeys are produced only in Ireland. They are a blend containing barley, malt whiskeys, and grain whiskeys. The malt, dried in coal-fired kilns without peat smoke, is triple-distilled. It is milder than single-malt Scotch (see below) and some blends.

Canada—Canadian whiskey is a blend distilled from rye, corn, and barley and is produced only in Canada under government control. It is lighter than American whiskey.

Gin

Gin is made principally in Holland, England, and America of a mixture of malt, corn, and rye. This mixture is fermented and distilled two or three times in pot stills and then combined with juniper berries for flavor. Most gin is colorless. Some gins that are aged in barrels have a light, golden color. The proofs vary from eighty to ninety-four.

Rum

Rum is distilled from molasses or sugarcane juice and is aged in uncharred barrels to pick up a little color. Caramel is added to create dark rums. Most rums are blends. They are diluted and bottled at eighty proof.

Vodka

The Russian word *vodka* is the diminutive for water. Originally made in Russia from potatoes, today vodka is more often distilled from corn and wheat in the United States. The differences among vodkas depend on the grains used and the distilling and filtering processes. Most U.S. vodkas are filtered through activated charcoal. Vodka is colorless, tasteless, and odorless and, therefore, is an ideal base for other spirits, liqueurs, and mixed drinks in which alcohol, but no other taste, is desired.

THE CREAM FACTOR

The addition of some kind of cream is the raison d'être of cream liqueurs. Reading about commercial liqueurs and reading their labels reveals that the cream consistency may be imparted by fresh Irish dairy cream, U.S. dairy cream, double dairy cream, or Australian dairy cream. Although cream is the basis, the cream is diluted with some proportion of milk or other product that is lower in butterfat. The presence of butterfat makes the drink creamy, but it also is partially responsible for the thickness and viscosity of the liqueur. The objective is to reduce the butterfat content in homemade liqueurs by adding products with less butterfat and to prevent the mix from thickening.

Creamy liqueur products, produced before 1979 and not labeled *cream*, were made with non-dairy products. Some companies continue to make delicious products using non-dairy cream; you'll find them among the mixed drinks rather than among hard liquors on your grocer's or liquor store's shelf. Because they do not contain real cream, they cannot be labeled as cream products although they resemble them in thickness, texture, and taste.

Fresh cream is physically and chemically complex. It is a milk formula in which the fat globules have become more concentrated than usual either by rising to the top in a bottle or by separating due to the action of a centrifuge. Because cream is a milk product it is as highly perishable as milk. Despite pasteurization, all fresh milk products contain bacteria and will sour quickly when not refrigerated.

In addition, the flavor of these fresh dairy products can be altered by the electrical energy carried in ordinary daylight. That's why most milk products are sold in heavy cardboard or dark glass containers. Whenever milk is stored in clear glass or plastic containers, it should be kept in the dark as much as possible. That's also the reason that commercial cream liqueurs are in brown bottles.

Three Grades of Cream, Milk

Three grades of cream are found at the dairy counter. Unfortunately the butterfat content is rarely marked and can only be obtained from the particular dairy that produced the cream. Approximate butterfat content of the three cream grades are as follows:

> Light cream—between eighteen and thirty percent butterfat
> Whipping cream—between thirty and thirty-six percent butterfat
> Heavy cream—between thirty-six and forty percent butterfat

By contrast, whole milk is about four percent butterfat. Half and half is between milk and cream and must be at least ten and one-half percent butterfat. There is also two percent milk and non-fat milk in addition to the canned milks discussed below. Chocolate milk is also available with different fat contents.

Cream provides a thick, smooth texture and rich taste and

can be whipped into a stable foam. Whipping cream can whip into a thick, airy, glorious foam. When it is stubborn, it can fail to whip and fall flat into its original, liquid state. Whipping cream, when it behaves properly, becomes whipped cream—a foam of air and water stabilized by the proteins contained in the liquid.

Light cream, whipping cream, and heavy cream should only be stirred and not beaten or blended on high speeds when making homemade liqueurs. You want to minimize the thickening process, not encourage it.

Condensed Milks

Condensed milk products are a concentrated form of milk. To the person who makes homemade cream liqueurs, their advantage is that they do not spoil as easily as fresh creams.

Evaporated milk or ordinary condensed milk is made by rapidly evaporating about half its water under a vacuum process—not by heating. The resulting liquid is sterilized so that it will keep indefinitely and then is homogenized. The process gives the liquid its slight beige color and caramel flavor. Once the canned milk is opened, it has about the same storage life as fresh milk. Evaporated milk is available in four percent milkfat and a two percent, low-fat product.

Sweetened condensed milk is different from evaporated milk in that the caramel flavor is replaced by a more intense sweetener. The addition of sugar to the condensed milk completely inhibits the presence of bacteria, so the mix should not spoil. This characteristic makes condensed milk a natural addition to homemade cream liqueurs, and its use yields a longer storage life than those made with only fresh milk and cream. It also acts as a sweetening agent and substitutes for the sugar syrup used in clear, non-cream liqueurs.

Watch for the following changes in measurement equivalents when you use canned milk:

A 14-ounce can of sweetened condensed milk is by weight, and one 13- or 14-ounce can = approximately 1 cup.

A 12-ounce can of condensed milk is by weight, and one 12-ounce can = approximately 1 cup.

THE EGG FACTOR

Eggs are a combination of yolk and albumen. They are such complicated materials that food science still has not uncovered the mysteries of their composition and their behavior when combined with other materials.

For the recipes in this book, eggs are used to hold the liquid ingredients together, that is, to prevent them from separating in some solutions. The eggs form some of the volume—as much as ¼ to ½ cup in the recipes.

Always use eggs cold from the refrigerator when you add them to the liqueur mix to keep them from whipping and to minimize the incorporation of air, which tends to thicken the liqueur. (Warm egg whites are recommended for baking because volume and airiness are desirable.)

Always add eggs last and use the slowest or lowest speed on the blender, perhaps the stir setting. Then pulse stir, which means turn the machine on and off about eight times in one minute for this final addition. This technique prevents excess air from being incorporated into the mixture and helps to prevent the liqueur from thickening.

Should you want to cut down on cholesterol, you can leave out the eggs, but the mixture may separate as it stands in the refrigerator. It won't affect the taste; simply shake or stir again before serving. To reduce calories, use less of the sweetened condensed milk and more evaporated or low-fat milk. The liqueur will not be as rich, but the flavor will be almost the same as the sweeter versions. When too much sweetened condensed milk is added, it overpowers the flavors; you begin to taste only the milk. Adjust recipes to your own taste. That's why making cream liqueurs is creative and challenging.

When recipes thicken too much, add more whole milk, two percent milk, or non-fat milk to thin. For chocolate-based drinks, you may add low-fat milk or vodka (or a clear liqueur base) to thin to desired consistency.

Other products, such as coconut milk or cream of coconut, help to stabilize a solution. When coconut milk is present, for example, eggs may be eliminated from the recipe. The same is true for fruits that contain pectin.

MAKING CLEAR LIQUEURS AS A BASE FOR CREAM LIQUEURS

The premise of this book is that one can make cream liqueurs from scratch—start to finish. The easiest, fastest route is to use commercial, clear liqueurs as the flavor base to which you add other spirits, cream, and eggs. However, you can also make the clear liqueurs yourself and then add the cream to the homemade varieties. We discussed clear liqueur making in great detail in our earlier book, *Homemade Liqueurs*, which offers more than fifty recipes, plus ways to use them (see Bibliography).

For those who have not delved into that exciting hobby (or seeming career to some, as our mail indicates), we offer in this book basic procedures and a few simple recipes for clear liqueurs. These recipes may be quickly and easily adapted by adding such enhancements as cream and additional flavors for new taste experiences. You'll find these in detail in Chapter 3.

Making clear liqueurs yourself is a definite economy; the costs for ingredients are easily one-half to one-fourth the cost of their commercial counterparts. The results are almost foolproof.

Creating clear liqueurs is as easy as steeping tea. The process is called *macerating* or *steeping*. It is a marinating process, in which flavors, fruits, and spices are soaked in vodka or brandy for a short time. Then a sweetening syrup, usually made of sugar and water boiled together, is cooled, and added to the liquor mixture.

The liqueurs that are the easiest to produce and most often used as a basis for cream liqueurs are those made with coffee, mint, vanilla, and almond. Fruit flavors may be made from fruit extracts or fresh fruits such as oranges and berries. The most popular recipes that best adapt to the addition of creams are included in Chapter 3.

Clear liqueurs do not provide as instant a result as cream liqueurs, but the wait is well worthwhile. Steeping time is needed for the flavors to be released into the spirits. The flavorings are then strained or filtered out of the spirits (like filtering coffee into a coffee pot), and the liquid is then sweetened and put away for a few weeks for final aging. Time spent making them is minimal; you can literally mix a batch of liqueur in minutes. It's the time spent waiting, not knowing what it's going to taste like, that creates anxiety.

Most often, the spirit base is vodka because it imparts only alcohol and no flavor. A plain brandy or a flavored brandy may be used if you wish to combine the original flavor with that of the brandy. Perhaps a blackberry brandy will greatly enhance and strengthen the taste of a berry-flavored liqueur base.

Clear liqueurs may be colored to simulate the color of the flavoring ingredient. For example, green food color can be added to crème de menthe; red can be added to a cherry or strawberry mixture.

Supplies You Will Need:

- A wide-mouth, one-gallon glass (*not plastic*) jar for steeping.
- Glass bottles, which have been washed and sterilized in a dishwasher, for storing. Examples are: beer bottles, glass Perrier bottles, or decorative liqueur or wine bottles with corks or screw-on lids.
- Measuring cups, strainers, coffee filters, and funnels.

Step-By-Step Procedures

1. Select the flavor or prepare the fruit as indicated. Place it in the one-gallon jar and pour vodka over it so the fruit is completely covered (use smaller jars for half-recipes); the fruit must be completely submerged in the vodka, not floating on top. Cover tightly and steep as indicated. Turn the jar upside down and shake it gently every few days during the steeping time.
2. Strain the fruit or flavoring. Then filter out fine particles using a coffee filter until the liquid is clear.
3. Prepare the sugar syrup (see below). Always cool the syrup *before* adding to alcohol, as heat dissipates alcohol. Whole sugar grains do not dissolve in alcohol, thus the need for sugar syrup.

Sugar Syrup

1 cup sugar
½ cup water

Combine sugar and water in heavy saucepan. Bring to boil; continue cooking, stirring constantly until sugar dissolves and a thin syrup results. Cool.
Makes about 1 cup sugar syrup

4. A maturing time is recommended. The finished liqueurs should be stored, tightly covered, in a cool, dark place for three to four weeks.

The same recipes offered for making clear liqueurs can become *crème de* liqueurs when extra sweetening is added. Generally, use two cups of sugar syrup, made by doubling the recipe for sugar syrup given above.

SHORTCUT TO MAKING
CLEAR LIQUEURS

The above method requires steeping, filtering, sweetening, and aging before the liqueurs are ready to drink or to mix with creams.

There is a shortcut. Several companies market small bottles of concentrated liqueur flavors. You have to provide the vodka or brandy and the sugar syrup. Concentrates may be purchased in gourmet food and wine shops, or by mail order from sources listed in magazines that cater to people who like to read about, cook, and consume gourmet foods.

3 Creating Cream Liqueurs

Ready? Gather your ingredients and plug in your blender. In a few minutes, you'll have your first batch of cream liqueur.

Begin with the combinations we suggest, then mix and match your own flavorings. The possibilities are infinite. If you are in doubt about what might taste good, ask yourself if a given fruit or flavoring will lend itself to mixing with cream or milk, or if it might make a good milk shake or ice cream flavor. If so, chances are it will make a good cream liqueur, too.

Remember to record the products and procedures used so you can readily duplicate a super-successful result and avoid repeating any that may be only so-so. Your notes may soon reveal a pattern based on your individual tastes. You will know what to change the next time. Our notes revealed that the brandy recipes were too strong for our liking, so we diluted the brandy with vodka. We also discovered that fruit recipes tasted better when part of the spirit was vodka.

From a taste viewpoint, there is little you can do to ruin a mixture. One recipe may be stronger or sweeter. Some may be thicker than you anticipated—especially those made with fresh fruits instead of more predictable extracts, syrups, or powders. Sometimes fruits differ by season, ripeness, and variety and will cause the mixture to be unexpectedly viscous.

You can begin to develop your own taste standards for spirits when you taste test commercial cream liqueurs one after another. Dominant flavors are chocolate and/or coffee. Obvious variables are the taste of the spirit base and the smoothness of the drink.

Buy two or three different brands. Pour each one in a separate teaspoon. Observe the color and viscosity and then smell and taste each one to begin to familiarize yourself with their similarities and differences. When you make and taste test your own, you'll know what you are looking for. If tastes mingle as you test, take a bite of crackers, a few nuts, or a sip of water between each sampling.

You will probably note that Häagen-Dazs, which is made with a combination of spirits and French cognac, has a milder taste than Waterford Irish Cream made with Irish whiskeys. Different tastes are to be expected. If they were alike, there would be no need for different varieties. Long live taste differences and people who prefer one flavor over another.

When you make your own cream liqueurs, the final taste is affected by the type and amount of flavoring; the freshness and variety of fruits; the brand of chocolate syrup, spirit, and evaporated or condensed milk; and the strength of a flavoring extract.

As you experiment, try half-recipes for testing. Or make full recipes, but alter the spirit combinations for half of the recipe until you discover which combinations you prefer.

If thickening occurs, thin down the liqueur by adding non-fat or low-fat milk, fresh or canned milk, vodka, or a ¼ cup or so (depending on how much liqueur remains) of the spirit initially used. Shake well or reblend. Always stir, shake, or whisk the liqueur before serving when it has been stored for several days.

Note: Sweetened condensed milk and evaporated milk are measured by weight and the number of ounces is marked on the cans. Large cans offered by different packagers vary; some contain thirteen ounces and others fourteen ounces. Either can yields approximately 1 cup. Use a half can or less for ½ cup. A five- or six-ounce can measures approximately ½ cup.

Do not worry about being absolutely exact in these measures; a half ounce, or one ounce, more or less won't make an appreciable difference in the recipes.

CREAM LIQUEURS MADE WITH FLAVORINGS AND RAW INGREDIENTS

Amaretto Cream Liqueur #1

   3 teaspoons almond extract
   1½ cups cognac
   ½ cup (7 ounces) sweetened condensed milk
   ½ cup (5-ounce can) evaporated milk
   2 eggs

Blend together extract and cognac in blender. Add milks and blend at low speed for 1 minute. Add eggs and pulse stir for 1 minute (use the lowest speed on blender and turn on-off eight times).
Makes approximately 3 cups

Amaretto Cream Liqueur #2

>1 cup toasted blanched almonds
>1½ cups brandy, cognac, whiskey, scotch, or rum
>½ teaspoon pure vanilla extract
>½ cup (5-ounce can) evaporated milk
>½ cup (7 ounces) sweetened condensed milk
>2 eggs, beaten

In a blender or food processor, grind almonds until fine. Add spirits and vanilla; blend. Add milks and blend at low speed for 1 minute. Add eggs and pulse stir for 1 minute (use the lowest speed on blender and turn on-off eight times). Tiny flecks of almonds add to the taste and flavor.

Makes approximately 3 cups

Coconut Cappuccino Cream Liqueur

>¾ cup brandy
>¼ cup vodka
>2 teaspoons chocolate syrup
>2 teaspoons cappuccino instant coffee
>½ cup (7 ounces) sweetened condensed milk
>¼ cup two percent milk
>½ cup cream of coconut

Combine ingredients and blend in blender for 5 minutes. Store in refrigerator. If mixture thickens, add non-fat or low-fat milk until desired consistency.

Makes approximately 3 cups

Double Chocolate-Chip Irish Cream Liqueur

1½ cups semisweet or sweet chocolate chips
2 cups Irish whiskey
3 tablespoons cocoa powder
1 cup (14-ounce can) sweetened condensed milk
1 cup chocolate condensed milk
2 eggs

Chop chocolate chips or broken pieces of block chocolate into tiny pieces in blender (reserve ¾ cup). Add whiskey and cocoa to remaining ¾ cup of chocolate, and blend in blender until mixed. Add milks and blend at low speed for 1 minute. Add eggs and pulse stir for 1 minute (use the lowest speed on blender and turn on-off about eight times). Add reserved chips so they float in liquid. *Note:* White chocolate may be substituted for or combined with dark chocolate.
Makes approximately 4 cups

Cognac-Base Cream Liqueur

This recipe simulates Häagen-Dazs.

1½ cups cognac
2 teaspoons instant coffee
1 teaspoon pure vanilla extract
1 teaspoon chocolate syrup
½ cup (7 ounces) sweetened condensed milk
½ cup (5-ounce can) evaporated milk
3 eggs

Add flavorings to cognac and blend in blender. Add milks and blend at low speed for 1 minute. Add eggs and pulse stir for 1 minute (use the lowest speed on blender and turn on-off eight times).
Makes approximately 4 cups

Irish Cream Liqueur #1

   1 teaspoon instant coffee (preferably a flavored Irish or
      cappuccino coffee)
   ½ teaspoon pure vanilla extract
   ¼ teaspoon almond extract
   2 cups Irish whiskey
   1 cup (14-ounce can) sweetened condensed milk
   4 large eggs

Add flavorings to whiskey and blend in blender. Add milk and blend on low speed for 1 minute. Add eggs and pulse stir for 1 minute (use the lowest speed on blender and turn on-off about eight times).

Makes approximately 4 cups

Irish Cream #2 (Extra Rich)

   1½ cups blended Irish whiskey
   1 teaspoon pure vanilla extract
   1 tablespoon instant coffee
   1 cup (12-ounce can) evaporated milk
   1 cup (14-ounce can) sweetened condensed milk
   6 eggs

Combine whiskey, vanilla, and coffee and blend in blender. Add milks and blend for 1 minute. Add eggs and pulse stir (use the lowest speed on blender and turn on-off about eight times) just until smooth and not thick.

Makes approximately 4 cups

Irish Cream #3 (without Eggs)

1½ cups rum
½ teaspoon instant Irish coffee powder
1 teaspoon pure vanilla extract
¼ teaspoon almond extract
1¼ cups light cream
1 cup (14-ounce can) sweetened condensed milk
¼ cup whole milk

Combine rum and flavorings and blend in blender. Add cream and milks and blend at low speed for 1 minute.
Makes approximately 4 cups

Mocha Chocolate Cream Liqueur

1 cup very strong coffee (liquid), cooled
3 teaspoons chocolate syrup
1½ cups bourbon
1 cup (14-ounce can) sweetened condensed milk
1 cup light cream
2 eggs

Blend coffee, chocolate syrup, and bourbon in blender. Add milk and cream. Add eggs and pulse stir for 1 minute (use the lowest speed on blender and turn on-off about eight times).
Makes approximately 4 cups

Mocha Coconut Rum Cream Liqueur

>1 cup very strong coffee (liquid), cooled
>1¼ cups rum
>¼ cup vodka
>1 cup (12-ounce can) evaporated milk
>¼ cup cream of coconut

Blend coffee, rum, and vodka in blender. Add milk and cream of coconut and blend until smooth.

Makes approximately 3½ cups

Orange-Chocolate Cream Liqueur

>1 teaspoon orange extract
>3 teaspoons chocolate syrup
>1½ cups brandy, scotch, or other whiskey
>1 cup (14-ounce can) sweetened condensed milk
>1 cup whipping or light cream
>3 eggs

Blend orange extract and chocolate syrup with spirits in blender. Add milk and cream and blend on low speed for 1 minute. Add eggs and pulse stir for 1 minute (use the lowest speed on blender and turn on-off eight times).

Makes approximately 4 cups

Vanilla Cream Liqueur

>1 cup sugar
>½ cup water
>3 teaspoons pure vanilla extract
>1 cup vodka
>1 cup brandy
>1 cup (12-ounce can) evaporated milk
>4 eggs
>1 vanilla bean

Combine sugar and water in saucepan, heat to boiling, and stir just until thickened. Cool completely. Combine vanilla, vodka, and brandy and blend in blender. Add cooled sugar syrup and blend. Add milk and blend at low speed for 1 minute. Add eggs and pulse stir for 1 minute (use the lowest speed on blender and turn on-off about eight times). Pour into bottle and add vanilla bean.

Makes approximately 4 cups

FRESH FRUIT RECIPES

Fresh fruits usually should be sliced and reduced to a liquid in the blender using a little of the spirits to help puree or liquify, if necessary. For a liqueur recipe that yields 4 cups, use ¾ cup to 1 cup pureed fresh fruit. Fruits have pectins that tend to thicken the mixture. They also have inherent sweetness. Therefore, recipes that call for fruit use less of the sweetened condensed milk than those made with extracts, coffee, and chocolate. To achieve a thinner drink (or one that does not thicken) use combinations of half and half, or two percent or non-fat milk and pulse stir only until blended. Overstirring and incorporating too much air into the mixture will cause it to thicken.

Eggs generally are not used with fresh-fruit based cream liqueurs as they tend to increase thickness or viscosity. (Recipes made with fresh juice may need eggs to prevent the mix from separating.) If you want the added richness of eggs, use them cold from the refrigerator, add them in last, and pulse stir only until mixed.

You may use any spirit base you like that seems appropriate with a fresh fruit in place of the ones we suggest. Use caution, though. Too much of a strongly flavored spirit overpowers the fruit. So, dilute the spirit with a portion of vodka, which does not add flavor.

Banana Cream Liqueur

    2 ripe bananas, mashed (about 1 cup)
    1 teaspoon pure vanilla extract
    1¼ cups whiskey
    ½ cup vodka
    ¼ cup (3½ ounces) sweetened condensed milk
    ½ cup (5-ounce can) evaporated milk
    ½ cup two percent or non-fat milk

Blend bananas with vanilla, whiskey, and vodka in blender. Add milks and pulse stir at low speed for 1 minute (use the lowest speed on blender and turn on-off eight times) or until smooth.
Makes approximately 4 cups

Banana Coconut Rum Cream Liqueur

    2 ripe bananas, mashed (about 1 cup)
    2 teaspoons coconut extract
    1½ cups rum
    ½ cup vodka
    ½ cup (3½ ounces) sweetened condensed milk
    ½ cup (5-ounce can) evaporated milk
    1 cup cream of coconut or coconut milk

Mash bananas and blend in blender with coconut extract, rum, and vodka. Add milks and blend at low speed for 1 minute. Add coconut and pulse stir for 1 minute (use the lowest speed on blender and turn on-off eight times).
Makes approximately 4 cups

Berry Cream Liqueur

    1 cup fresh or frozen blueberries, drained (or a
        combination of berries in season)
    1 teaspoon pure vanilla extract
    1 cup blackberry-flavored brandy
    ½ cup vodka
    ½ cup (7 ounces) sweetened condensed milk
    ½ cup (5-ounce can) evaporated milk
    ½ cup half and half

  Puree berries in blender. Then blend with vanilla, brandy, and
vodka. Add milks and half and half and blend at low speed for 1
minute.
Makes approximately 4 cups

Cherry Cream Liqueur

    ½ pound pitted fresh cherries, pureed
    1½ cups American whiskey
    ½ cup vodka
    ¼ cup (3½ ounces) sweetened condensed milk
    ½ cup (5-ounce can) evaporated milk
    ¼ cup whole milk
    1 drop red food coloring

  Add cherries to spirits and blend in blender. Add milks and food
coloring and pulse stir for 1 minute (use the lowest speed on blender
and turn on-off eight times). Add more red food coloring, if
necessary, until color is pleasing.
Makes approximately 4 cups

Kiwi Cream Liqueur

> 6 medium-size kiwifruit peeled, sliced
> 1½ cups American whiskey
> ½ cup vodka
> ¼ cup (3½ ounces) sweetened condensed milk
> ½ cup (5-ounce can) evaporated milk
> ¼ cup whole milk
> Green food coloring

Add sliced, peeled kiwi to spirits and blend in blender. Add milks and one drop of food coloring and pulse stir for 1 minute (use the lowest speed on blender and turn on-off eight times). Add an additional drop of green food coloring or more, if necessary, until the mixture is a pleasing green color.

Makes approximately 4 cups

Mango Cream Liqueur

> 1 cup fresh mango, pureed
> 1 cup vodka
> ½ cup American whiskey
> ½ cup (7 ounces) sweetened condensed milk
> ½ cup (5-ounce can) evaporated milk
> ½ cup two percent milk

Blend mango with vodka and whiskey. Add milks and blend at low speed for 1 minute.

Makes approximately 4 cups

Orange (Triple Sec) Cream Liqueur

1 cup sugar
½ cup water
1 cup fresh orange juice
¾ cup whiskey (any kind)
½ cup vodka
1 teaspoon cinnamon
1 teaspoon ground cloves
¼ cup whole or low-fat milk
1 egg

Combine sugar and water in saucepan, heat to boiling, then simmer and stir until blended and mixture forms a light syrup. Cool completely. Blend orange juice, whiskey, vodka, cinnamon, and cloves in blender. Add cooled sugar syrup and blend ½ minute. Add milk and blend at low speed for 1 minute. Add egg and pulse stir 1 minute (use the lowest speed on blender and turn on-off eight times).
Makes approximately 4 cups

Peach Cream Liqueur

2 to 3 fresh, medium-size peaches unpeeled, sliced, and
    with pits removed to yield 1 cup puree
1½ cups American whiskey
½ cup vodka
¼ cup (3½ ounces) sweetened condensed milk
½ cup (5-ounce can) evaporated milk
½ cup two percent milk

Puree peaches in blender. Add whiskey and vodka and blend. Add milks and blend at low speed 1 minute. *Note:* When peaches are in season, they can be pureed with a little vodka and frozen in ice cube trays or plastic cups. To make peach liqueur when fruit is out of season, thaw cubes and make above recipe.
Makes approximately 4 cups

Strawberry Cream Liqueur

    1½ cups sliced, fresh strawberries
    1 teaspoon milk
    2 teaspoons pure vanilla extract
    1 cup American whiskey
    ½ cup vodka
    ¼ cup (3½ ounces) sweetened condensed milk
    ½ cup (5-ounce can) evaporated milk
    ¼ cup whole or low-fat milk

Combine sliced strawberries in blender with 1 teaspoon milk to puree. Add vanilla, whiskey, and vodka and blend. Add milks and blend at low speed for 1 minute. The strawberry particles will appear in the liqueur.

Makes approximately 4 cups

RECIPES USING COMMERCIAL CLEAR LIQUEURS

The cream liqueur combinations that are possible when using a commercial clear liqueur as a base are limited only by the varieties you have available and how they taste with cream. Remember, if the flavor sounds likely for a milk shake, it will probably be delicious as a cream liqueur. If it doesn't appear likely, try a sample by creating a drink of one part liqueur to three parts cream to determine whether it appeals to your taste buds. For example, we weren't sure about melon (Midori) and cream, but a sample convinced us it was as good as honeydew or cantaloupe with a heaping spoon of ice cream in the middle.

Basic Recipe #1: Cream Liqueurs Made with Commercial Clear Liqueurs

1¼ cups favorite liqueur such as amaretto, Grand
Marnier, Cointreau, Kahlùa, mint, chocolate,
coconut, cassis, Sabra, vanilla, banana, peach,
cherry, strawberry, and so on. The flavors may be
combined to create delicious alliances such as
chocolate-mint and chocolate-coconut.

¼ cup another flavor or type of spirit such as whiskey,
rum, or gin

1 cup (14-ounce can) sweetened condensed milk

1 cup whipping or light cream or evaporated milk

2 or 3 eggs

Combine all ingredients except eggs in blender on low speed until
smooth, 1 to 2 minutes. Add eggs and pulse stir for 1 minute (use the
lowest speed on blender and turn on-off eight times). Store in
refrigerator up to one month.

Makes approximately 4 cups

Amaretto Cream Liqueur #3

1¼ cups amaretto liqueur (commercial or homemade
with vodka base)

½ cup gin

1 cup (14-ounce can) sweetened condensed milk

1 cup whipping cream or light cream

3 eggs

Blend together liqueur, gin, milk, and cream until smooth. Add
eggs and pulse stir 1 minute (use the lowest speed on blender and
turn on-off eight times).

Makes approximately 4 cups

Kahlùa-Mint Irish Cream Liqueur

1¼ cups Kahlùa
¼ cup Irish whiskey
2 teaspoons peppermint extract
1 cup (14-ounce can) sweetened condensed milk
1 cup whipping or light cream
2 eggs

Combine Kahlùa, whiskey extract, milk, and cream and blend 1 to 2 minutes in blender. Add eggs and pulse stir 1 minute (use the lowest speed on blender and turn on-off eight times).
Makes approximately 4 cups

Midori Cream Liqueur

1½ cups Midori liqueur
¼ cup whiskey
1 cup (14-ounce can) sweetened condensed milk
1 cup half and half
2 eggs

Combine liqueur, whiskey, milk, and half and half and blend in blender at low speed for 1 minute. Add eggs and pulse stir 1 minute (use the lowest speed on blender and turn on-off eight times).
Makes approximately 4 cups

Wishniak Cream Liqueur

1¼ cups cherry liqueur
¼ cup bourbon
1 cup (14-ounce can) sweetened condensed milk
1 cup whipping or light cream
2 eggs

Combine cherry liqueur, bourbon, milk, and cream, and blend 2 to 3 minutes in blender. Add eggs and pulse stir 1 minute (use the lowest speed on blender and turn on-off eight times).
Makes approximately 4 cups

Basic Recipe #2: Cream Liqueurs Made with Commercial Crème de Liqueurs

Remember that *crème de* refers to a liqueur that is sweeter than a plain liqueur but is still a clear liqueur. A *cream* liqueur requires the addition of cream or milk. But because *crème de* liqueurs already have additional sweeteners, use less of the sweetened condensed milk than when using commercial clear liqueurs. Follow the same recipe as Basic Recipe #1 (page 49), except reduce sweetened condensed milk to ½ cup (7 ounces) instead of 1 cup (14 ounces).

Chocolate Mint Cream Liqueur #1

> 1 cup mint liqueur (non-cream) such as crème de menthe, Gold-O-Mint, Vandermint, or homemade mint liqueur
> 1½ cups blended whiskey
> 2 teaspoons chocolate extract
> ½ cup (7 ounces) sweetened condensed milk
> 1 cup (12-ounce can) evaporated milk

Combine all ingredients in blender and blend 1 to 2 minutes.
Makes approximately 4 cups

Crème de Cassis Cream Liqueur

> 1 cup crème de cassis
> 1½ cups cognac
> ½ cup (7 ounces) sweetened condensed milk
> 1 cup (12-ounce can) evaporated milk
> 1 egg

Combine all ingredients except egg in blender and blend 1 to 2 minutes. Add egg and pulse stir 1 minute (use the lowest speed on blender and turn on-off eight times).
Makes approximately 4 cups

Crème de Banana Cream Rum Liqueur

1 cup crème de banana
1 cup rum
½ cup (7 ounces) sweetened condensed milk
1 cup (12-ounce can) evaporated milk
½ cup no-fat milk
1 egg

Combine all ingredients in blender except egg and blend 1 to 2 minutes. Add egg and pulse stir 1 minute (use the lowest speed on blender and turn on-off eight times).
Makes approximately 4 cups

Crème de Strawberry Cream Liqueur

1 cup crème de strawberry
½ cup pureed fresh strawberries
1½ cups whiskey
½ cup (7 ounces) sweetened condensed milk
1 cup (12-ounce can) evaporated milk
1 egg

Combine all ingredients in blender except egg and blend 1 to 2 minutes. Add egg and pulse stir 1 minute (use the lowest speed on blender and turn on-off eight times).
Makes approximately 4 cups

MAKE YOUR OWN CLEAR LIQUEURS—THEN ADD CREAM

Making clear liqueurs is similar to steeping tea: soak flavorings in spirits, add sugar syrup, and age the mixture in dark bottles or in light bottles in a dark cabinet. To avoid aging time, you may wish to use commercially prepared concentrated liqueur flavors. They are packaged complete with recipes. Generally, you need only add sugar syrup plus vodka and they do not require refrigeration. A more complete discussion of clear liqueur making is found in Chapter 2. In addition, our earlier book, *Homemade Liqueurs*, provides more than fifty recipes for clear liqueurs (see Bibliography).

After the clear liqueur is aged, filtered, and finished, add spirits, cream, milk, and egg as in the above recipes made with commercial clear liqueurs. After creams are added, the products require refrigeration.

The ratio is generally:

> 1¼ to 1½ cups clear liqueur
>
> ¼ to ½ cup other spirit: whiskey, gin, bourbon, rum, cognac, etc.
>
> ½ or 1 cup sweetened condensed milk (depending on sweetness and thickness desired)
>
> ½ to 1 cup other milks (again depending on thickness of previous ingredients)
>
> 1 to 3 eggs to add richness and to act as an emulsifier or stabilizer for the ingredients. Always use eggs cold and pulse stir for 1 minute (use the lowest speed on blender and turn on-off eight times)

Note that fresh fruits used in making clear liqueurs are left whole or sliced; they are not pureed. The fruits are filtered out of the clear mixture. The recipes will yield 3 to 4 cups clear liqueur unless otherwise noted. Only 1½ cups clear liqueur are required as the base for a 4 cup cream liqueur recipe. The shelf life of clear liqueurs is much longer than for cream liqueurs. We have kept some for more than a year and they still taste great. Or, make half recipes only for a 2 cup yield.

One more note: you cannot re-create the commercial varieties of clear liqueurs with any more success than you can the cream liqueurs. You can only *simulate* Kahlùa, Grand Marnier, or Vandermint, for example. So recipes given are not for the *brand*, but are for a combination of flavors often used in these well-known liqueurs.

Basic Sugar Syrup Recipe for Clear Liqueurs

> 1 cup sugar
> ½ cup water

Heat sugar and water together in saucepan. Bring to boil; continue cooking, until sugar dissolves and a thin syrup results. Cool.
Makes 1 cup

Fresh Apricot Liqueur

> 1 pound fresh apricots
> 3 cups vodka
> ½ cup water
> 1 cup sugar

Cut unpeeled apricots in half and remove pits. Place pits in a plastic or paper bag and hit them with a hammer to open. Remove inner nut and discard pit covers. Place nuts in a bag and hit them to crush and release flavorful oils. (Any remaining trace of pit covering can impart a bitter taste.) Combine the fruit and nuts in vodka. Steep 2 weeks. Shake gently 2 or 3 times a week. Strain and squeeze all juice from fruit. Filter until clear. Boil together water and sugar in saucepan to make syrup (see recipe above). Cool and add to mixture. Mature 2 to 3 months. Use as a base for cream liqueurs.
Makes approximately 4 cups

Fresh Berry Clear Liqueurs

The advantage of making clear liqueurs with fresh berries is that you can capture their in-season freshness. Then, you can use the clear liqueur as the base for cream liqueurs at any time of the year and in quantities that are compatible with your drinking and cooking needs.

Use freshly picked berries if possible. You can use one type of berry such as strawberry, blueberry, raspberry, huckleberry, or combine different varieties. Frozen berries may be used, too. Note that they are usually softer and more watery than fresh berries. Use less sugar syrup when making liqueurs from frozen berries to avoid diluting the alcohol.

4 cups fresh berries
Sliced and scraped peel of one lemon or lime
Pinch of tarragon or cloves
3 cups vodka or 2 cups vodka and 1 cup brandy or
    sweet white wine
1 cup sugar
½ cup water

Lightly crush berries with a fork. Add to vodka with lemon or lime peel and tarragon or cloves. Steep 3 months. Strain. Crush the berries through a filter to squeeze out all juices. Heat sugar and water in saucepan. Bring to boil; continue stirring until sugar dissolves and a thin syrup results. Cool and add to filtered liquid. Mature 3 weeks.
Makes approximately 5 cups

Crème de Cassis

1 cup black currants (or substitute raisins)
2½ cups brandy or vodka
2 cups sugar
1 cup water

Place currants in alcohol in a tightly closed jar and steep for 1 week. Shake jar occasionally during the week. Strain and filter. Heat sugar and water in saucepan. Bring to boil; continue stirring until sugar dissolves and forms a light syrup. Cool and add to filtered liquid. Mature 2 weeks.
Makes approximately 4 cups

COFFEE LIQUEURS

The Mexican Kahlùa and Jamaican Tia Maria are the names usually associated with coffee liqueurs, although other companies market coffee flavors under a variety of names. Mixing coffee-flavored liqueur to keep on your shelf for drinking and to use as a cream liqueur base can become a career in itself.

The basic coffee liqueur can be the host for other flavors such as mint, orange, or chocolate. Those combinations can be varied by adding different spirits. Try it with Irish, Canadian, Australian, and American whiskeys; with gin, bourbon, and rum; or with vodka alone. You can change the creaminess of the concoction by using milks with different butterfat contents for richer, sweeter, or not-so-rich, not-so-sweet combinations. Optional additions are pinches of cinnamon, cocoa, cloves, orange peel, cardamon, and mint leaves or extracts such as coconut and cherry.

And finally, you can change the flavor and strength of the coffee base by using different instant coffees in different amounts. You will find Irish, cappuccino, and mint instant coffee, as well as other exotic flavors, available on your grocer's shelf.

Basic Recipe for Coffee Liqueur

> 2 cups water
> 2 cups sugar
> ¼ to ½ cup dry instant coffee (fresh jar)
> 1 vanilla bean
> 1½ cups vodka
> Caramel coloring (optional)

Make sugar syrup by boiling water and sugar in a saucepan until dissolved. Turn off heat. Slowly add dry instant coffee and continue stirring. Add a chopped vanilla bean to the vodka, then combine the cooled solution of sugar syrup and coffee with the vodka in a large jar. Cover tightly and shake vigorously each day for 3 weeks. Strain and filter. Add caramel coloring if desired.
Makes approximately 4 cups

Chocolate Liqueur

As a liqueur flavor chocolate is ubiquitous. There are so many ways to use chocolate in cream liqueurs that a chocoholic's eyes will gleam. In the majority of cream liqueurs it is used by itself or with coffee.

Making the basic chocolate clear liqueur yourself and then adding creams will considerably reduce the cost of liqueur making. Chocolate-flavored liqueurs need not use expensive vodka. Adding a good or high grade of Irish whiskey or other spirit will yield an incomparable base for added creams. The greater the butterfat content of the milk product, the richer the mix.

Some combinations you may be familiar with are chocolate coconut, chocolate mint, chocolate cherry, chocolate strawberry, chocolate peanut, and chocolate coffee.

Basic Recipe for Chocolate Liqueur

¼ cup water
½ cup sugar
2 teaspoons pure chocolate extract
½ teaspoon pure vanilla extract
1½ cups vodka

Heat and stir water and sugar in saucepan until sugar dissolves and thin syrup results, to make ½ cup recipe of sugar syrup. Cool. Add all other ingredients and mix well. Let mature several days. Then use as a base for cream liqueurs. *Note:* Chocolate liqueurs may be made with chocolate syrup and powdered cocoa, but they have a weaker flavor than extract and a residue forms in the bottle which cannot be eliminated. However, when making a cream liqueur, chocolate syrup and cocoa may be added to the mix because they dissolve in the cream.
Makes approximately 2 cups

Coconut Liqueur—Clear or with Cream

> 2 cups brandy
> 12-ounces flaked coconut or fresh coconut cut into
>   small chunks
> 1 teaspoon coconut extract
> ½ teaspoon pure vanilla extract
> For cream liqueur:
> ½ cup (7 ounces) sweetened condensed milk
> ½ cup whole milk

Combine brandy, coconut, and extracts in bottle and let steep 3 to 4 weeks. (Does not need to be refrigerated.) Shake the bottle every 3 to 4 days. Strain out coconut through coffee filter or cheesecloth. (For the basic clear coconut liqueur, sugar syrup may be required, but add only 1 or 2 ounces at a time and taste test.)

For the cream liqueur: do not add sugar syrup as the coconut milk acts as both a sweetener and a thickener. Add the milks and blend in blender at low speed for 1 minute.

Makes approximately 3 cups

NUT LIQUEURS

A variety of clear liqueurs have nuts as their flavor basis. Almonds are the flavor in amaretto, hazelnuts are the basis of Crème de Noisette, and walnuts are the basis of Crème de Noix. Liqueurs have appeared on the market made with peanuts, pistachio nuts, and combinations of nuts with other flavorings.

Amaretto is the most popular nut liqueur. Reading the labels on commercial cream liqueurs reveals that almonds are often one of the "varied flavorings" added to the proprietary recipes. Following are two basic ways to create amaretto, or almond clear liqueur, which you can mix with other liqueurs or use as a basis for amaretto cream. If you like the flavor of other nuts, substitute them for the almonds, or make a mix of walnuts, almonds, and other nuts (do not use salted varieties). Liqueurs can be made from the nuts themselves or from extracts.

Almond Liqueur Made with Extract

¼ cup water
½ cup sugar
1 teaspoon pure almond extract
1½ cups vodka

Heat and stir water and sugar in saucepan until sugar dissolves and forms a light syrup. Cool. Add to extract and vodka. Shake well. Mature a few days and it is ready to drink or to mix with creams.
Makes 2 cups

Chopped Fresh Almond Liqueur

Select whole, fresh, natural (unblanched and unsalted) almonds and chop them coarsely with a knife, in a nut chopper, or in a food processor. Chopping releases the flavorful oils that will permeate the vodka. Do not chop them too fine or the mix will be hard to filter.

3 ounces whole, unblanched and unsalted, fresh
    almonds
1½ cups vodka
Pinch of cinnamon
¼ cup water
½ cup sugar

Chop nuts coarsely and add to vodka and cinnamon. Shake well and steep about 2 weeks, shaking every few days. Filter. Heat and stir water and sugar in saucepan until sugar dissolves and forms a light syrup. Cool. Add to vodka mix. Shake well and store 2 to 3 more weeks before using.
Makes 2 cups

ORANGE LIQUEURS

Orange peels are used as the flavoring for most commercially produced orange liqueurs. But, when you make them at home, you can use orange juice, orange extracts, and whole oranges. Commercial varieties differ in the ingredients combined with the basic orange and spirit base. Grand Marnier, for example, uses cognac but the same recipe can be used with vodka.

Simulated Grand Marnier

> 3 cups cognac
> Pinch of cloves
> Pinch of nutmeg
> 1 cup sugar
> ½ cup water

Peel oranges, always scraping the white rind from the peels as it can impart a bitter flavor to the liqueur. Cut peel into large chunks. Steep orange peels 2 to 3 weeks in cognac. Strain and filter. Heat and stir sugar and water in saucepan until sugar dissolves and forms a light syrup. Save pulp for another use. Cool. Add to filtered liquid. Mature 4 to 6 weeks and it is ready for use.
Makes approximately 4 cups

4 Cocktails, Coffees, and Ice Creams

Devilishly decadent might be an apt description for the addition of cream liqueurs to cocktails and coffees. They can be used as a sauce for ice creams. But, you also can sandwich, or layer them, between ice creams, whipped cream, fruits, and cream. You'll never want to be without some flavor of liqueur in the refrigerator when that urge for something sweet comes over you. Never again will you have to ruminate over what to serve guests when you're determined to make your menu different and delicious.

The recipes that follow are idea stimulators. Use them to help you brainstorm ways you can use fruit juices, coffees, or anything else with cream liqueurs in uncanny, uncommonly good combinations.

Among the tried and true liquids that wed naturally with liqueurs are coconut milk, pineapple juice, orange juice, chocolate drinks, clear liqueurs of almost any flavor, soda, and carbonated drinks such as 7-UP, colas, ginger ale, Sprite, and others.

The liqueurs used in the recipes in this chapter that are italicized are homemade from recipes given in Chapter 3. Note that flavors may be substituted to taste and commercial liqueurs may be used. All recipes are for one serving unless otherwise indicated.

Think of adding cream liqueurs to punch, too. It makes an eggnoglike brew that can be served year-round.

To help increase your cream liqueur mixing repertoire, peruse recipes in bartending books. Note that many use a plain liqueur and call for the addition of cream. Instead of using the two ingredients separately, substitute a homemade or commercial cream liqueur in an amount equal to the combined amount of the liqueur and cream in the recipe.

WHEN TO SERVE CREAM DRINKS

Brunch

Cream liqueurs, because of their milk-cream content, are an excellent choice for brunches. Milk coats the stomach and will soothe and slow the absorption of liqueur into the blood stream. Straight liqueur is absorbed more quickly when there is no food in the stomach; that explains why people become intoxicated faster when they drink on an empty stomach. Cream liqueurs made with orange juice, pineapple juice, or mixed with fresh or canned fruits can be a dramatic drink for early-in-the-day dallying.

Midday to Late Afternoon

Midday. Ah—a time when a cream drink can be gratifying and relaxing. Any day, but especially on a hot day, mix cream liqueur with ginger ale or soda and serve over crushed ice with a colorful cocktail straw poked in. It will be sip-able and satisfying as the ice melts. The creamy sugar drink is a perfect pick-me-up for reviving energies and softening the edge of late-afternoon hunger pangs. The diluted alcohol content will be low enough to assuage fears of drunk driving, too. A midday to late afternoon drink over crushed ice in a brandy glass encourages slow sipping and swirling. What could be nicer?

Desserts

After lunch or dinner, the undiluted drink served in a cordial glass, can be a dessert in itself. If you wish to linger over dessert, serve the drink over crushed ice to make a frappé. Or make a blender drink with ice and fresh fruit such as strawberries, pineapple, or peaches and serve in a cocktail glass. Garnish with whole fruit.

Need more proof of their versatility? Cream liqueurs can be served as an accompaniment or mixed into the coffee cup, too. That's being super chic—more modern than serving espresso or demitasse. But, do use the small cups for company. It's surprising and fun.

After Dinner

Liqueurs are a traditional after-dinner drink. Place several bottles on a tray with glasses nearby and encourage guests to select their own favorite flavors.

Bedtime

At bedtime when you need something fresh, soothing, and smoothing, cream liqueurs can be the perfect answer. Milk is a sleep inducer itself, and, for insomnia, the added spirit can work better and taste better than any medicine.

HOW TO SERVE—GLASSES AND GARNISHES

Cream liqueur drinks are appetizing by their very nature. But you add splendor by dressing them up in appropriate glasses and with garnishes. You don't have to be a purist about the type of glass used. If a stemmed water glass is the right size to enhance the drink's appearance, use it.

A variety of nicely shaped glasses can be used for drinks, ice cream concoctions, fruits with liqueur on top of them, parfaits, pudding—even cheesecakes. The drinks are new. No established precedents exist for which kind of drink belongs in which glass.

When serving drinks and desserts with liqueurs and ice creams, you generally use small glasses rather than large glasses. Or, if using large glasses, fill them with ice or whipped cream. The ingredients are rich, strong, and filling so you don't want to serve too much.

Use eye catching, creatively prepared garnishes for eye and appetite appeal. It is nice if the garnishes reflect the ingredients of the drink, but it's not essential. A strawberry perched on the rim of a strawberry cream liqueur drink acts as a taste and visual tie-in. For a pineapple coconut drink (piña colada) place a chunk of each fruit on a skewer and serve. Here are other possibilities:

Half a strawberry on edge of glass leaving the stem on

Orange, lemon, or lime peel curls

Orange, lemon, or lime slice with the edges notched. Notch the whole fruit before slicing by cutting narrow wedges from the skin vertically from tip to tip.

Orange and lime slice together, folded on a toothpick or skewer

Slice of banana with a cherry in front

Mint or other leaves

Pineapple and coconut chunks with cherry on a toothpick

Cinnamon sticks

Vanilla bean

Kiwifruit slice

Skewered blueberries, raspberries, or both

Purple grapes, skewered

Cherry and pineapple wedge

Attractive straws

Dollop of whipped cream with cinnamon on top

Dollop of whipped cream with shaved chocolate on top

Shaved chocolate on a frothy blended drink

Whipped cream with an additional liqueur whipped in for
  another flavor
Slivered almonds
Cinnamon, nutmeg, or powdered, flavored instant coffee
  sprinkled on whipped cream

MIXING HINTS

Mixed drinks call for stirring, shaking, and blending. It's also
a good idea to shake the bottle before you mix a cream liqueur
with other ingredients.

Stirring the ingredients with ice usually is accomplished
with a bar spoon, with the back of the spoon against the glass.
This spins the ice in the middle of the drink. Then you can
remove the ice with the spoon and serve in the same glass. Or,
if you're making large quantities, stir the ice and drink mixture
in a large mixing jar and pour into individual glasses.

For stirring fizzes and floats, use a small wire whip and
blend the liquids to create a light foamy drink.

Shaking is accomplished in a two-part shaker that consists of
a metal bottom with a glass or metal top. Place the ingredients,
with ice, in the metal bottom. Tilt the metal and place the glass
part on top. (Don't put the top on while the metal bottom is
straight up and down or they will be hard to separate.) Tap the
top gently to create a snug fit. Grab the shaker with both
hands so each hand is on the bottom surface of one shaker
part. Raise the shaker near your right shoulder and vigorously
shake it back and forth about ten times until the metal feels
cold.

Separate the two parts with the metal on the bottom. Place
a bar strainer over the metal rim and pour the liquid into a
glass.

Blending refers to placing the liquids in an electric blender,
with or without ice, using a mix, blend, or whip speed. The
result will be a foamy, frothy drink. Ice helps dilute and thin
the liquid; adding soda or plain milk will also thin the drink.
When ice is added, use the bar strainer over the mixer bowl
and pour the drink into a glass.

FRAPPES

A frappé is any liquor served over finely crushed ice. A stemmed cocktail glass or champagne glass is used.

Traditional Frappé

> 3 ounces cream liqueur (any flavor)
> ¼ cup crushed ice

Place crushed ice in a cocktail glass. Pour liqueur over it. Serve with a straw.

Double Frappé

> 2 ounces cream liqueur (any flavor)
> 1 ounce clear liqueur or fruit juice
> ¼ cup crushed ice

Place crushed ice in a cocktail glass. Mix the two liqueurs (or liqueur and juice) and pour the mixture over crushed ice. Garnish and serve with a straw.

Floats

A float consists of one or more liqueurs, a scoop of ice cream, and a compatible soda such as root beer, club soda, ginger ale, 7-UP, etc. This works well in an 8-ounce water glass and is pretty in a stemmed water glass.

Peachy Cream Float

> 2 ounces *peach cream liqueur* (page 47)
> 1 scoop peach ice cream
> 4 to 6 ounces ginger ale

Pour liqueur in glass, add ice cream. Fill with ginger ale.

Chocolate Cow Float

2 ounces *double chocolate-chip Irish cream liqueur*
(page 39)
1 scoop chocolate ice cream
4 to 6 ounces root beer

Pour liqueur in glass, add ice cream. Fill with root beer.

Fizzes

A fizz is a base cream liqueur poured over ice with club soda, ginger ale, 7-UP, or root beer added and gently stirred with a bar spoon or wire whip. Usually served in an 8- or 10-ounce highball glass with a straw.

Mocha Coconut Rum Fizz

1½ ounces *mocha coconut rum cream liqueur* (page 41)
½ ounce *Kahlùa-mint Irish cream liqueur* (page 50)
3 ice cubes
6 ounces ginger ale

Pour liqueurs over ice cubes in glass. Add ginger ale. Gently stir with spoon to fizz.

Favorites from Famous Bars

We asked bartenders for their favorite recipes and following are takeoffs of creamy editions of already well-known cocktails.

Kiwi Colada Hopper

1½ ounces *kiwi cream liqueur* (page 46)
1½ ounces coconut milk
3 ice cubes

Combine ingredients in blender at low speed until cubes are broken, then for 1 minute on whip setting. Strain and pour into a stemmed cocktail glass or champagne glass.

Irish Piña Colada

3 ounces *Irish cream liqueur* (page 40)
1½ ounces coconut milk
1½ ounces crushed pineapple
(or substitute 3 ounces fresh coconut-pineapple drink
    for the coconut milk and crushed pineapple)

Mix ingredients together in blender for 1 minute. Serve over ice in a brandy snifter or old-fashioned glass or in any cocktail glass without ice, if preferred. If desired, garnish with chunks of skewered pineapple and coconut, with cherry on top for color.

Irish Mint Cream

¾ ounce clear crème de menthe liqueur
1½ ounces *Irish cream liqueur* (page 40)
Whipped cream
Chocolate shavings
Kiwifruit slice

Pour clear crème de menthe in bottom of glass. Slowly add *Irish cream liqueur* down inside of glass to form a second layer. Add whipped cream so it mounds above glass rim. Garnish whipped cream with chocolate shavings. Do not stir; the liqueurs will subtly blend into one another, but keep their distinct tastes as they are consumed. Place kiwifruit slice over edge of glass. Serve with spoon or spoon and straw.

Banana Bonanza

   1 ripe banana
   2 ounces Häagen-Dazs Cream Liqueur or homemade
      cognac-base cream liqueur (page 39)
   1 ounce lime juice
   6 ounces crushed ice
   Whipped cream

Cut banana into 6 to 8 small pieces and place in blender with other ingredients except whipped cream. Blend at low speed, then higher speed for a total of 2 minutes. Pour into glass and garnish with whipped cream.

Häagen-Dazs Dreamberry

   1 ounce Häagen-Dazs Cream Liqueur or *cognac-base*
      cream liqueur (page 39)
   1 ounce clear crème de cacao
   1 ounce sliced or frozen strawberries
   2 ice cubes
   Strawberry

Blend liqueur, crème de cacao, strawberries, and ice together in blender until smooth. Pour into a stemmed glass. Garnish with a strawberry.

Cherry Flip

   1 ounce *cherry cream liqueur* (page 45)
   1½ ounces rum
   1 egg
   3 ounces crushed ice
   Nutmeg or cinnamon

Place in shaker or jar with lid. Shake well. Strain into glass. Garnish with nutmeg or cinnamon.

Strawberry Coconut

> 2 ounces *strawberry cream liqueur* (page 48)
> 2 ounces cream of coconut
> 2 ounces crushed ice
> Strawberry

Place all ingredients except strawberry in blender. Use high setting and blend until frothy, about 2 minutes. Pour into glass and garnish with a strawberry.

Olla Podrida

> 4 ounces of any flavors of cream liqueurs mixed
>   together
> 2 ounces crushed ice

Olla Podrida is a Spanish phrase for a stew all mixed in one pot. Use any combination of ingredients, or make an Olla Podrida drink when you have small amounts or many flavors of cream and clear liqueurs left over. The recipe is for one glass, but you can make a blender full or add the mixture to a punchbowl to pack a taste wallop.

COFFEES

Coffee with liqueur has long been a favorite drink, but the addition of cream liqueurs makes coffee super delectable; the cream provides a richness and body that complements the coffee. Top the coffee with whipped cream and garnish with chocolate curls, cinnamon, or a sprinkle of flavored instant coffee powder.

For superb extra flavoring, use any of the wide range of new, flavored, instant coffee products on the market. You'll find cappuccino, amaretto mocha, Irish cream, orange cappuccino, and so on.

Check the grocer's shelves frequently as new products and flavors appear. Mix flavored coffees with any homemade or commercial cream liqueurs. Drink them hot. Or keep a jar of strong coffee in the refrigerator and use it for iced coffee and cream liqueur combinations. Almost any go well together. Cold coffees are wonderfully refreshing in hot weather. They are perfect for the final touch at a brunch or a luncheon or for sipping as you lounge around a pool or spa.

Hot Irish Coffee

1½ ounces *Irish cream liqueur* (page 40)
6 ounces hot black coffee
Whipped cream

Add liqueur to coffee. Top with whipped cream. Do not stir. Sip the coffee through the whipped cream.

Häagen-Dazs Caribbean Rum

1½ ounces Häagen-Dazs Cream Liqueur or homemade
   cognac-base cream liqueur (page 39)
½ ounce white rum
4 ounces hot coffee
Whipped cream

Combine liqueur, rum, and coffee. Top with whipped cream.

Mocha Warmer

1 ounce Häagen-Dazs Cream Liqueur or homemade
   cognac-base cream liqueur (page 39)
1 ounce Kahlùa or a homemade *coffee liqueur* (page 56)
6 ounces strong hot coffee
Whipped cream

Combine liqueurs with coffee. Top with whipped cream.

Creamy Cappuccino

2 tablespoons instant cappuccino coffee powder
4 ounces hot water
1½ ounces *cognac-base cream liqueur* (page 39) or *Irish cream liqueur* (page 40)

Dissolve powder in hot water. Add liqueur. Top with whipped cream.

Cold Chocolate Mint Mocha

2 ounces *double chocolate-chip Irish cream liqueur* (page 39)
8 ounces strong cold black coffee
1 ounce *Kahlùa-mint Irish cream liqueur* (page 50)
2 ice cubes or 3 ounces crushed ice

Mix all ingredients in blender and serve in a tall glass with a straw.

Kahlùa-Mint Coffee

1 ounce *Kahlùa-mint Irish cream liqueur* (page 50)
1 cup steaming black coffee
Whipped cream

Add liqueur to coffee. Top with whipped cream.

Peach Yogurt Coffee

3 ounces plain or peach yogurt
3 ounces cold black coffee
2 ounces *peach cream liqueur* (page 47)
2 ice cubes or 3 ounces crushed ice
Cinnamon

Mix yogurt (reserve some for garnish), coffee, liqueur, and ice in blender and serve in a tall glass with a straw. Add a dollop of yogurt on top and sprinkle with cinnamon.

Iced Amaretto Café

2 heaping teaspoons amaretto mocha instant coffee
4 ounces hot water
Ice cubes
2 ounces *amaretto cream liqueur* (page 37)
Whipped cream
Slivered almonds

Dissolve amaretto mocha instant coffee in hot water. Pour over ice cubes to cool. Add liqueur. Whip mixture slightly with wire whip. Serve over ice cubes in a tall glass with a straw. Garnish with whipped cream and slivered almonds.

ICE CREAMS WITH CREAM LIQUEURS

Mix cream liqueur with ice creams for one phase of dessert making. Then, pour more liqueur over the ice cream and it's a double whammy of wonderful tastes.

You can be even more creative by adding liqueur-blended ice creams as a layer or two in a parfait, dropping a couple of ounces into a milk shake or malt, or by using them for a topping on sundaes. Your reputation as a dessert creator extraordinaire will be sweetened. This section contains ideas that will whet your appetite. Non-dairy whipped topping may be substituted for whipped cream.

To blend cream liqueurs into ice cream, or dairy whipped topping, thaw ice cream or topping slightly until soft. Gradually pour liqueur into cream and gently stir to blend. Refreeze ice cream or refrigerate non-dairy cream.

Irish Kiwi Parfait

>2 ounces *kiwi cream liqueur* (page 46)
>Vanilla ice cream
>1 ounce *Irish cream liqueur* (page 40)
>2 chocolate wafer cookies crumbled
>Whipped cream
>2 green maraschino cherries

Pour 1 ounce *kiwi cream liqueur* in bottom of glass. Add a layer of vanilla ice cream, a layer of 1 ounce *Irish cream liqueur*, a layer of crumbled chocolate cookies, a layer of 1 ounce *kiwi cream liqueur*. Fill with ice cream to ½ inch below glass top. Mound whipped cream on top. Garnish with green cherries.

Baked Apple A-La-Orange-Mode

>½ pint vanilla ice cream
>3 tablespoons *orange cream liqueur* (page 47)
>4 large baking apples
>4 cinnamon sticks
>Cinnamon, powdered
>4 ounces Sprite (or any soft drink)

Soften ice cream and mix with liqueur. Refreeze. Core apples and pare skin from one end. Place unpared end down in baking dish. Insert 1 cinnamon stick in each apple. Pour soft drink evenly over apples. Sprinkle cinnamon on pared portion of each apple. Bake, covered, in 350°F oven for 45 minutes or until apples are soft. Let cool. To serve, place a scoop of ice cream on each apple.
Serves 4

Peachy Creamy Dessert

1 ounce *peach cream liqueur* (page 47)
3 ounces canned or fresh peaches cut into small pieces
Vanilla ice cream, slightly softened
½ cup crushed ice

Blend all ingredients in blender until creamy. Pour into a tulip or champagne glass.

Cherry Chocolate Dream Parfait

2 ounces *cherry cream liqueur* (page 45)
1 scoop chocolate ice cream
10 fresh cherries, pits and stems removed
1 cup crushed ice
2 tablespoons chocolate ice cream
Stemmed cherries
Chocolate curls

Blend liqueur, 1 scoop ice cream, cherries, and ice on high speed in blender until creamy. Fill parfait glass halfway with liquid. Add 2 tablespoons ice cream, then fill glass with remaining liquid. Garnish with stemmed cherries and chocolate curls. Serve with long-handled parfait spoon.

Liqueur-Blended Ice Cream in Chocolate Cups

Buy ready-made chocolate candy serving cups. Mix ice cream with any flavor cream liqueurs. Serve in chocolate cups and garnish. Chocolate cups are edible, of course.

Häagen-Dazs Cream Cassis Soda

1½ ounces Häagen-Dazs Cream Liqueur or *cognac-base*
      cream liqueur (page 39)
¾ ounce *crème de cassis currant liqueur* (page 55)
½ cup crushed ice
Soda

Place crushed ice in tall soda glass, add liqueurs and soda, stir
briskly with a spoon.

Orange-Amaretto Sherbet Refresher

1½ ounces *orange cream liqueur* (page 47) or Cointreau
      with cream added
4 ounces fresh squeezed orange juice
1 teaspoon almond extract
1 scoop sherbet, any flavor
Orange slice

Mix liquids. Place in tall glass and add sherbet. Garnish with
orange slice.

5 Cakes and Cheesecakes

Liqueurs can impart subtle flavorings to cake batters, fillings, and toppings. Add them to batters you make yourself or add them to prepared cake mixes to make the ordinary extraordinary. The only caution? Don't overdo. If you follow a few simple procedures, you'll have perfect results every time.

When enhancing cakes, pies, and cookies, the liqueur should be subtle—not overpowering. A minimum of two tablespoons of a cream liqueur is needed or the added flavor may not be discernible. More likely, ¼ to ½ cup of liqueur is required before the taste is evident.

Alcohol tends to dissipate during long periods of baking. Cakes to be baked forty-five minutes to an hour require the addition of ¼ to ½ cup of liqueur. For cakes with a short baking time, a smaller amount of liqueur will impart detectable flavoring. Keep notes on how much you add to a particular recipe, its baking time, and how pronounced the liqueur is in taste.

ABOUT WHIPPING CREAM, HEAVY CREAM

When you add liqueurs to whipped cream, sour cream, cream cheese, or yogurt, one tablespoon of liqueur will impart a subtle taste to about six to eight ounces of the food. Begin with that amount and taste it. If it's not strong enough, add more. Note the amount of the addition and your taste results. Remember that some cream liqueurs will be stronger than others depending upon the spirit used for the base.

Stores sell *heavy* cream, *whipping* cream, and *light* cream. Check the butterfat content if marked. The higher the butterfat, the heavier the cream. Heavier creams whip and hold up better.

For best whipping results, whipped cream should be well-chilled. It can be placed in the freezer for ten minutes or so before whipping. Place the beaters and bowl in the freezer, too. Use an electric mixer for whipping a full container of whipped cream. A large wire whip works well with small amounts.

Whip the cream, then add the cream liqueur a little at a time. Usually the liqueur will impart flavor and sweetening to the whipped cream. But, if more sweetening is required, use powdered sugar rather than granulated sugar, although both will work. Granulated sugar has a greater water content than powdered sugar. Thus, it tends to melt into the cream and cause an undesirable separation process.

ABOUT EGGS

Separate whole eggs. Beat liqueurs into yolks with a mixer at low speed or with a wire whip. Fold them into beaten, stiff egg whites.

Egg whites should be beaten at room temperature, because they achieve a greater volume when slightly warm. This is especially important for soufflés and sponge cakes where volume is required. Warm eggs by placing them in a bowl of warm water about ten minutes before using. (You want the eggs to be cold in the liqueur recipes themselves to prevent them from adding volume and thickening the solution.)

Whole eggs separate best when they are cold. Store extra egg whites in the freezer. Place the white from each egg in one cube mold of an ice cube tray. When frozen, turn them out and place in a plastic bag or storage container and return to freezer. When you need egg whites, you'll have them ready to use. To hasten thawing or warming, place on defrost in microwave for a few minutes until whites are at room temperature.

Egg yolks can be stored for about a week in the refrigerator. Store in a glass container and cover the yolks with a little vegetable oil. Then, cover the glass with foil.

ABOUT CHOCOLATE

Many recipes call for melted chocolate. Chocolate has its own set of characteristics. When you respect them, you'll be successful with your first melting effort. Ignore the principles and you'll meet with failure and frustration.

Two cautions: do not overheat and do not have a single drop of water in the container in which you melt the chocolate. If the chocolate does become obstreperous, add about a teaspoon of vegetable oil or melted shortening for every two ounces of chocolate. Beat vigorously until the chocolate responds and resumes the desired consistency.

Four possible methods for melting chocolate are as follows:

1. Place the chocolate in the top pan of a small double boiler over hot water. The pan holding the chocolate must be completely dry. Heat until chocolate warms and appears to have a film on top. Remove from heat. (The chocolate doesn't lose its shape and appear to melt unless it is overheated.) Stir until smooth and proceed with the recipe.
2. Place the pan with chocolate inside a larger pan containing hot, but not boiling, water, and stir as it melts. This apparatus is called a *bainmarie*.

3. Place chocolate in a bowl and heat at defrost temperature in a microwave oven. Ovens and temperatures differ, so experiment until the chocolate melts properly.
4. Large amounts of semisweet, sweet cooking, and milk chocolate can be melted and kept at a dipping consistency using a temperature-controlled Crockpot. Unsweetened chocolate tends to become too liquid.

When other ingredients are to be melted with the chocolate:

- Milk or butter added to chocolate hastens the melting process. If you melt these ingredients in a pan directly over very low heat (as opposed to a double boiler), stir and watch it as it heats. Chocolate continues to melt after it is removed from the heat, so melt it partially, remove from heat, and stir until smooth.
- Adding liqueurs to chocolate can sometimes cause the chocolate to thicken or ball up. If this happens, smooth mixture by adding vegetable oil or melted shortening.
- White chocolate should be grated to encourage even melting. White chocolate varies among brands, so you will have to experiment with the type you have available. If white chocolate tightens, add a small amount of boiling water and it will probably become smooth.

ADDING LIQUEURS TO CAKE RECIPES

The general procedure is to mix the liqueur into the whipped cream, non-dairy topping, cream cheese, or yogurts or fold into beaten egg whites. Then, use those ingredients in the same quantities called for in the recipe.

For sponge cakes and pound cakes, poke holes in the baked cakes and drop liqueur into the holes with a poultry baster. Icings, custards, and sauces are perfect vehicles for cream liqueurs on cakes.

The liqueurs used in the recipes in this chapter that are italicized are homemade from recipes given in Chapter 3. Note that another flavor or a commercial cream liqueur may be substituted.

No-Bake Strawberry-Chocolate Mosaic Cake

A rum-based cream liqueur containing any kind of berry can be used, but strawberries are the showiest.

8 ounces semisweet chocolate
¼ cup *strawberry cream liqueur* (page 48)
8 ounces butter
3 tablespoons powdered sugar
2 eggs, separated
1 cup chopped walnuts
6 ounces shortbread-style cookies
2 pints fresh strawberries or blueberries

Melt chocolate in top of double boiler. Stir in liqueur and let cool to room temperature.

Beat and cream together butter and sugar. Beat and add egg yolks one at a time. Mix in walnuts. Add cooled chocolate mixture.

In small deep bowl, beat egg whites to form soft peaks. Break cookies into about ½-inch squares and fold into beaten egg whites. Gently fold this mixture into the chocolate batter mixture until equally distributed.

Lightly oil an 8½" × 4½" loaf pan. Spoon half of chocolate batter into pan. Smooth surface. Pat dry one half of the strawberries and space them on surface of batter evenly. Add remaining chocolate batter. Smooth top. Chill four hours. Before serving, invert on serving platter and decorate by placing remaining strawberries in rows on top of cake.

Note: This recipe may be doubled and made in a 10-inch round springform cheesecake pan.

Serves 10 to 12

Chocolate Mocha Marnier Roll

    5 eggs, separated
    ¾ cup powdered sugar
    ¼ cup *mocha chocolate cream liqueur* (page 41)
    ¾ cup sifted cake flour
    ¾ teaspoon baking powder
    ½ teaspoon salt
    3 tablespoons unsweetened cocoa powder
    3 tablespoons powdered sugar

    Filling and frosting:
    2 cups whipping cream (yield 4 cups whipped cream)
    3 tablespoons *orange cream liqueur* (page 47)
    2 cups chopped walnuts
    4 cherries

Grease bottom and sides of a flat, jelly-roll cake pan 15½″ × 10½″ × 1″ with vegetable oil or butter. Preheat oven to 350°F.

Prepare cake batter. In a small mixing bowl, beat egg yolks until thick and lemon-colored about 5 minutes. Gradually add ¾ cup powdered sugar. Gradually mix in liqueur until blended.

Sift cake flour before measuring ¾ cup. Resift into large bowl with baking powder, salt, and cocoa powder. Add flour mixture gradually to egg mixture and beat until smooth.

In a large mixing bowl, beat egg whites until soft peaks form (do not overbeat). Lightly fold egg whites into egg flour mixture. Spoon into pan and spread gently until even.

Bake 15 to 18 minutes until cake barely springs back when pressed with fingertip. Loosen edges as soon as cake is taken from oven. Roll while warm, using the following procedure:

Spread smooth cotton towel on large breadboard. Sprinkle towel with 3 tablespoons powdered sugar (just barely coat it to prevent cake from sticking). Spread towel tautly over cake pan, then place breadboard on top of towel. Turn over so cake inverts onto towel. Remove cake pan.

Starting at narrow end, roll cake with towel into a loose roll. Cool rolled-up cake on wire rack for about 1½ hours.

Whip cream until soft peaks are formed. Gently fold in orange liqueur. Spread waxed paper on work area. Carefully unroll cooled cake onto waxed paper while removing towel. Spread cake with half the whipped cream. Roll loosely like a jelly roll using the waxed paper to help roll, but *do not roll* waxed paper into cake. With a spatula, place a thin layer of whipped cream on outside of cake. Sprinkle coating of chopped nuts on waxed paper and lift paper so nuts adhere to whipped cream. Finish decorating top of cake with whipped cream. Garnish with cherries. Refrigerate at least 3 hours. May be frozen.

Serves 8 to 10

Bundt Cake with Coconut Cream Liqueur Custard

½ cup *coconut cream liqueur* (page 58)
1 package yellow Bundt cake mix
Shredded coconut
Maraschino cherries

Prepare custard (included in cake mix) and stir in *coconut cream liqueur*. Prepare cake mix and bake according to package directions. Spread with icing. Decorate with shredded coconut and maraschino cherries.

Serves 10 to 12

Strawberry Ice Cream/Liqueur Angel Food Cake

1 package angel food cake mix or ready-made angel
    food cake
2 pints strawberry ice cream
1 cup *strawberry cream liqueur* (page 48)
1 pint fresh strawberries

Prepare angel food cake batter and bake according to package directions. Cool cake and remove from pan. Remove ice cream from freezer and put in large bowl until thawed so you can stir it with a wooden spoon. Add *strawberry cream liqueur* to ice cream and blend with wooden spoon. Return to freezer until the ice cream is rethickened to spreading consistency—not frozen. Slice strawberries, reserving some whole strawberries for decorating the cake.

Pour liqueur into holes made in the cake with skewers and slice cake into layers, as shown. Use toothpicks and a ruler to measure layers so they will be evenly cut. Work quickly. Spread ice cream on layers, add sliced strawberries, and reassemble. Place in freezer to reharden as you work, if necessary. Coat top with ice cream and refreeze whole cake. Remove from freezer about 15 minutes before ready to slice and serve. Place fresh, whole strawberries on top.
Serves 10 to 12

Chocolate Chip Cookie Cake

½ cup milk
1 cup *chocolate liqueur* (page 57)
1 pound chocolate chip cookies
1 large (12-ounce) container non-dairy whipped
    topping
Shaved chocolate

Combine milk and ½ cup of the liqueur in a soup bowl. Dip each cookie into mixture and line bottom of 8½" × 11" cake pan with layer of cookies. Mix remaining ½ cup liqueur with whipped topping. Spread layer of topping over cookies. Put another layer of dipped cookies on topping, reserving some cookies to make crumbs. Cover with second layer of topping. Crush remaining cookies to make crumbs and garnish with crumbs and shaved chocolate curls. Refrigerate at least 4 hours. Cut in squares to serve.

Serves 16 to 20

Refrigerator Banana Butterscotch Chiffon Cake

1 package lady fingers or 1 sponge cake
1 cup *banana cream liqueur* (page 44)
1 cup butterscotch chips
4 tablespoons water
6 eggs, separated
Whipped cream

Line 8½" × 11" cake pan with lady fingers or cake slices cut so pieces stand up around edge of pan to create scalloped effect. Drizzle ½ cup liqueur over lady fingers or cake. Melt chips. Add water. Beat in 6 egg yolks, one at a time. Beat egg whites until stiff. Fold butterscotch mixture into egg whites. Pour into cake pan. Chill. Whip cream and add in ½ cup liqueur. Cover cake. Refrigerate.

Serves 12 to 15

Dragon-Shape Amaretto
Chocolate Icebox Cookie Cake

2 packages chocolate wafers
1 container (12 ounces) non-dairy topping
1 cup *amaretto cream liqueur* (page 37)
8 ounces toasted slivered almonds
2 green, round candy gumballs
3 to 4 lengths of red licorice strips
Aluminum foil

Use a double layer of aluminum foil and shape a trough wide enough for diameter of chocolate cookies. Place on cookie sheet for support. Let non-dairy topping thaw to stirring consistency and mix in cream liqueur. Use topping as a mortar to hold cookies together for dragon's body. Spread each cookie with topping and place one end next to the other until the row can be shaped with the foil into an S-curve in the shape of a dragon. As you near the tail end, break cookies in half to taper the shape. Place in freezer for 2 or 3 hours to harden. Return extra topping to refrigerator.

When hard, remove from freezer and cover with remaining topping. Use rim of whiskey glass lightly pressed into top of dragon to simulate scale design. Stand a slivered almond at tip of each scale. Add gumballs for eyes, licorice for tongue and dragon's breath. Refreeze to harden. Remove excess foil and place on serving tray. Let thaw about 15 minutes before serving.
Serves 16 to 20

Blueberry Bonanza

    2 tablespoons butter
    2½ cups graham cracker crumbs
    ½ cup softened butter
    1 cup powdered sugar
    2 eggs
    1 can (21-ounce) blueberry pie filling
    ½ cup *berry cream liqueur* (page 45)
    1 cup chopped pecans or walnuts
    1 cup whipping cream
    2 tablespoons *berry cream liqueur* (page 45)

Melt 2 tablespoons of butter in 9-inch square cake pan. Pat 1½ cups of crumbs evenly over cake pan bottom. In a small bowl, beat ½ cup butter until fluffy. Add sugar gradually and beat until light and fluffy. Add eggs and blend well. Pour mixture slowly over crumb layer. Mix pie filling with liqueur and spread over butter-sugar mixture. Sprinkle nuts over blueberry filling. Whip cream and add liqueur. Spread evenly over filling. Sprinkle remaining graham cracker crumbs over top. Cover and chill for 8 hours. Cut into squares to serve.

Note: This recipe can be made with any flavor pie filling and a compatible flavor cream liqueur.

Serves 8 to 10

CHEESECAKES

Cream liqueurs are a perfect flavor enhancer for cheesecakes. Many traditional recipes already call for flavoring with clear liqueurs; the added ingredients from cream liqueurs produce a richer, smoother flavor.

Be as imaginative and inventive as you dare. Cream liqueurs can be added to the crusts and toppings of cheesecakes as well as to the fillings. And, any of the recipes can have crusts, fillings, or toppings mixed or matched as your mood, and available ingredients, dictate. Consider, too, how the flavors will round off a meal. Cheesecakes are a rich dessert and deserve the limelight. Serve them to cap off a simple dinner rather than to add richness to a heavy dinner already laden with sauces and calories. Cheesecakes are at their very best when served with coffee or tea for a midafternoon break or when dessert and drinks are suggested.

A few notes about cheesecake preparation will make every cake a success and will win rave reviews for the baker.

Basic Method for Preparing Cheesecakes

Cheesecakes are deceptive. Given their beauty and spectacular taste, they are surprisingly easy to make. You will need a cheesecake or springform pan, one in which the bottom can be freed from the sides. There are eight-inch, nine-inch, and ten-inch sizes with sides ranging in height from one and one-half to three inches. Use the eight-inch or nine-inch pan for recipes calling for twelve to sixteen ounces of cream cheese (three-quarters to one pound). Use the nine-inch or ten-inch pan with higher sides for recipes calling for four, eight-ounce packages of cream cheese (two pounds). If you plan to transport the cake and leave it somewhere, substitute the bottom metal round with a piece of cardboard covered with heavy-duty foil and a round of parchment.

Use ingredients at room temperature. Beat the cheese with the sugar and add the liqueur and other flavorings. Then add eggs one at a time with mixer on a low setting to prevent excess air from being beaten into the batter and affecting the texture of the cake. If ingredients are not at room temperature, the batter will be lumpy, but it will smooth during baking. Add an extra five minutes to the baking time when cold ingredients are used. Do not grease the bottom or sides of the pan. Bake at 350°F.

When baking is finished, the cake usually will pull away from the sides of the pan. But, if necessary, free it by dipping a knife or spatula in water and sliding it around the cake between the crust and the pan. Open the lock on the pan and slip the bottom with the cake out. Never try to lift the cake off of the bottom piece and place it on another serving platter.

After baking, place the cake in the refrigerator immediately to prevent cracks. Bake one or two days before serving and allow to settle in the refrigerator. Remove from refrigerator two to three hours before serving; cheesecakes taste best at room temperature. Do not use plastic wrap or foil to cover the cake in the refrigerator as they cause condensation and moisture collects on the cake topping. Store it in a cardboard box like those used by a bakery. If a cheesecake is refrigerated in the pan, cover the top with a cardboard round. Cheesecakes, with the exception of those made with chocolate, can be frozen successfully for several weeks.

When decorating cheesecakes, use a garnish that coordinates with the flavor.

Cheesecake recipes can combine cream cheese and cottage cheese and may be mixed in a blender or food processor. Tofu may be substituted for cheese.

Crust Recipes

Crusts can be made of sweet crumbs such as graham crackers, vanilla wafers, chocolate chip cookies, zwieback, Arrowroot tea biscuits, amaretto biscuits, gingersnaps, spiced wafers, and pecan sandies. The cookies or biscuits can be reduced to fine crumbs in a food processor or blender, or by placing the cookies in a plastic bag and rolling with a glass or rolling pin. Other ingredients can be added such as crushed almonds, walnuts, or pecans; grated chocolate; chocolate chips; butterscotch chips; grated coconut; wheat germ; brown sugar; and instant flavored coffee powder.

Add three to six tablespoons melted butter or margarine to the crumb mixture and press firmly into bottom or bottom and sides of pan. A tablespoon of cream liqueur may be added to the mix or sprinkled over the crust after it is pressed into the pan. The crust may be baked for five to eight minutes at 350°F, or it may be refrigerated until butter hardens.

8- or 9-inch Crust

For crusts for an 8- or 9-inch pan holding a 1-pound cheesecake use the following quantities:

1¼ cups crumbs
3 tablespoons melted butter
¼ cup sugar (optional depending on sweetness desired)

9- or 10-inch Crust

For crusts for a 9- or 10-inch pan holding a 2-pound cheesecake the quantities are the same as above when you plan to cover the bottom only with crumbs. When bottom and sides are to be covered use:

2¼ cups crumbs
5 to 6 tablespoons butter
¼ cup sugar (optional)

Toppings

A traditional cheesecake topping consists of sour cream, sugar, and a flavoring. But the richness and calories can be reduced by replacing one half of the sour cream with non-fat yogurt or a flavored yogurt such as blueberry, strawberry, or chocolate. Two to three tablespoons of cream liqueur may then be added to the topping.

Spread topping on top of cheesecake approximately ten minutes after cake is removed from oven. The cake may be baked an additional ten minutes or put into the refrigerator immediately.

Häagen-Dazs Creamy Cheesecake

Crust:
1¼ cups vanilla wafers, finely crushed
3 tablespoons butter, melted

Filling:
2 pounds (four packages, 8 ounces each) cream cheese
1 cup sugar
4 large eggs
1 teaspoon pure vanilla extract
½ cup *cognac-base cream liqueur* (page 39) or Häagen-
   Dazs Cream Liqueur

Topping:
1 cup sour cream
3 tablespoons sifted powdered sugar
¼ cup *cognac-base cream liqueur* (page 39) or Häagen-
   Dazs Cream Liqueur

Prepare crust. Mix wafer crumbs and melted butter. Pat in bottom
of 9- or 10-inch springform pan. Refrigerate.

Prepare filling. Preheat oven to 350°F. Beat cream cheese in large
bowl until smooth, scraping bowl as needed. Beat in sugar gradually.
Beat in eggs one egg at a time. Stir in vanilla and liqueur. Pour into
crumb crust. Bake about 1 hour and 10 minutes until knife inserted
1-inch from center of cake comes out clean.

Prepare topping. Mix sour cream, sugar, and liqueur until smooth.
Remove cake from oven and spread topping mix over cake top, bake
10 minutes more. Loosen edges of cheesecake with knife dipped in
water. Cool to room temperature in pan. Refrigerate at least 4 hours
or overnight. Remove from pan. Garnish with fruit.
Serves 16 to 20

Courtesy of Hiram Walker, Inc.

Dona's Easy Irish Cream Liqueur Cheesecake

Crust:
1¼ cups graham cracker crumbs
3 tablespoons melted butter

Filling:
1 pound (two 8-ounce packages) cream cheese
½ cup granulated sugar
½ cup *Irish cream liqueur* (page 40)
½ teaspoon pure vanilla extract
3 eggs

Topping:
8 to 12 ounces sour cream
2 teaspoons sugar
2 tablespoons *Irish cream liqueur* (page 40)
16 large fresh strawberries, hulled
1 cup sugar
3 tablespoons cornstarch
¾ cup water
2 drops red food coloring

Prepare crust by mixing crumbs and butter and pressing crumbs on bottom and sides of 8-inch cheesecake or springform pan. Press with palm of hand or bottom of glass. Refrigerate.

Prepare filling. Preheat oven to 350°F. Beat cream cheese and sugar in large bowl. Add eggs one at a time and beat at low speed. Stir in liqueur and vanilla and beat at low speed until smooth. Pour into crust. Bake 30 minutes or until knife inserted near center comes out clean. Remove from oven and cool on rack for 10 minutes.

Prepare topping. Mix sour cream, sugar, and liqueur until blended and spread mixture on top of cheesecake. Refrigerate. About an hour before serving garnish by placing two large strawberries on each slice.

Prepare glaze. Stir sugar and cornstarch together in medium-size saucepan. Gradually stir in water and cook over medium heat, stirring constantly until mixture thickens and boils. Add 2 drops food coloring and boil and stir 1 minute. Cool. Pour glaze over top of whole cheesecake or over individual slices just before serving.
Serves 8 to 10

Kiwi-Flavored Cheesecake

Crust:
1 cup vanilla wafer crumbs
½ cup grated semisweet or unsweetened chocolate
3 tablespoons melted butter

Filling:
1 pound (two 8-ounce packages) cream cheese
½ cup *kiwi cream liqueur* (page 46)
½ teaspoon pure vanilla extract
¼ cup sugar
3 eggs

Topping:
12 ounces sour cream (or 8 ounces sour cream and 4
    ounces unflavored yogurt)
¼ cup sugar
2 tablespoons *kiwi cream liqueur* (page 46)

Garnish with 3 kiwifruit, sliced

Prepare crust. Mix crumbs and grated chocolate with melted butter and press into 8-inch springform pan. Bake 5 minutes at 350°F. Remove from oven and cool.

Prepare filling. Preheat oven to 350°F. Beat cream cheese and add liqueur, vanilla, and sugar. Beat in eggs one at a time. Pour mixture into cooled crust. Bake 30 minutes. Cool 10 minutes.

Prepare topping. Blend sour cream, liqueur, and sugar and spread over cake top. Refrigerate for several hours. Before serving, garnish with sliced kiwifruit.

Serves 8 to 10

Double-Chocolate Coffee Cheesecake

Crust:
2¼ cups chocolate wafer crumbs
1 tablespoon instant mocha chocolate coffee powder
5 tablespoons melted butter
¼ cup sugar

Filling:
2 pounds (four 8-ounce packages) cream cheese
1 cup sugar
¼ cup *double chocolate-chip Irish cream liqueur* (page 39)
3 ounces chocolate, melted
2 teaspoons instant mocha chocolate coffee powder
½ teaspoon pure vanilla extract
4 large eggs
½ cup grated white chocolate or chocolate chips

Topping:
2 cups sour cream
¼ cup sugar
½ teaspoon vanilla
2 tablespoons double *chocolate-chip Irish cream liqueur*
   (page 39)
1 ounce semisweet chocolate, melted

Garnish with dark chocolate shavings or curls

Prepare crust. Mix ingredients and press into bottom and sides of 10-inch springform cake pan. Refrigerate.
   Prepare filling. Preheat oven to 350°F. Beat cream cheese and sugar. Add liqueur, melted chocolate, coffee powder, and vanilla. Beat in eggs one at a time at low speed. Fold in grated chocolate or chocolate chips. Bake 45 minutes. Remove cheesecake from oven and let stand 10 minutes.
   Prepare topping. Mix sour cream, sugar, vanilla, and liqueur until smooth. Add melted chocolate. Spread on slightly cooled cake. Garnish with chocolate shavings or curls. Refrigerate.
Serves 12 to 16

Amaretto Chocolate Cheesecake

Crust:
1 cup crushed coconut cookie bars
1 cup crumbled macaroons
½ cup crumbled chocolate-chip cookies
5 tablespoons butter
1 ounce unsweetened chocolate

Filling:
6 ounces semisweet chocolate
4 ounces (½ of an 8-ounce package) almond paste
½ cup *amaretto cream liqueur* (page 37)
1½ pounds (three 8-ounce packages) cream cheese
½ cup sugar
4 eggs
½ cup whipping cream

Prepare crust. Combine cookie crumbs to make 2¼ cups (save ¼ cup for filling). Melt butter and chocolate in small saucepan. Mix with crumbs. Spread and pat down crumb mixture in bottom and around sides of 9-inch springform pan. Refrigerate until hard.

Prepare filling. Preheat oven to 350°F. Melt chocolate and cool slightly. Cut almond paste into small pieces and place in mixer bowl. Beat at low speed, gradually adding liqueur. Beat until well blended. Set aside. In large bowl, beat cream cheese until smooth. Add sugar and blend well. Add in eggs one at a time and blend. Add almond paste mixture. Add cooled chocolate and beat until blended. Add whipping cream. Mix until smooth. Fold in remaining ¼ cup crumbs. Pour into crust. Bake 45 minutes. Cake center will be soft but will become solid as it cools. Refrigerate.

Serves 12 to 15

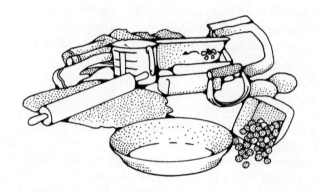

6 Pies, Filled Pastries, and Fruit Dishes

Cream liqueurs can accompany the ingredients in many of your successful pie recipes—especially those containing fillings that are compatible with milk and eggs. Mousse, puddings, gelatin desserts, and many fruit fillings may be enhanced by cream liqueurs.

Vary your piecrust recipes, too, by adding one of the following to the dough before rolling: 1 tablespoon poppy or caraway seed, 3 tablespoons toasted sesame seed, $\frac{1}{8}$ teaspoon cinnamon or nutmeg, 1 teaspoon grated citrus rind, 1 table-spoon sugar, $\frac{1}{4}$ to $\frac{1}{2}$ cup finely chopped nuts.

Make the dough yourself using a basic one or two piecrust recipe. For fast pie making, use prepared pie dough mix or a formed frozen ready-to-bake piecrust.

You can also prepare crumb crusts such as those used for cheesecakes (pages 89–90).

The liqueurs used in the recipes in this chapter that are italicized are homemade from recipes given in Chapter 3. Note that you may substitute another liqueur flavor or a commercial cream liqueur.

PIES AND FILLED PASTRIES

Basic Pie Dough Recipe

1½ cups all-purpose flour, sifted
½ teaspoon salt
½ cup shortening at 70°F or about room temperature
3 tablespoons water

Preheat oven to 425°F. Sift together flour and salt. Work in shortening with pastry blender until the grain in the mixture is the size of peas. Stir in water 1 tablespoon at a time until mixture holds together when you gather it into a ball. Roll it out into a flat circle, then place in pie pan and pat evenly. Pierce with fork tines in a few places to prevent crust from puffing. Bake 12 to 15 minutes. Cool before filling.
Makes one 9-inch crust. Double recipe for a two-crust pie.

Irish Cream Coffee Custard Pie

Crust for Double-Chocolate Coffee Cheesecake
    (page 94)
1½ cups chocolate wafer cookies, crumbled
Pinch of cinnamon
½ teaspoon instant Irish coffee powder
6 tablespoons unsalted butter, melted

Custard filling:
1¾ cups milk
¼ cup *Irish cream liqueur* (page 40)
6 egg yolks
2 tablespoons cocoa powder
2 tablespoons instant coffee powder
⅔ cup granulated sugar
2 envelopes unflavored gelatin
1 cup heavy cream
2 tablespoons *Irish cream liqueur* (page 40)
Chocolate shavings

Prepare crust. Preheat oven to 350°F. Mix all ingredients. Pat and press mixture firmly over the bottom of a 10-inch pie pan and 1½ inches up its sides. Bake 5 minutes.

Prepare filling. Add ¼ cup liqueur to milk and scald in a saucepan. In another saucepan, stir together egg yolks, cocoa, coffee, and sugar. In a cup or small bowl, dissolve the gelatin in hot water. Slowly pour the hot, scalded milk into the egg yolk mixture and stir until mixed. Place saucepan over low heat and stir until the mixture thickens and becomes a custard. (Do not allow to simmer.) Remove from heat, add gelatin, and stir until smooth. Strain the mixture through a sieve.

Assemble pie. Refrigerate custard to cool, but watch it carefully and stir frequently to prevent setting. When the custard appears to be about ready to set, whip the heavy cream to soft peaks and gently whip in the liqueur (reserve about ¼ cup for rosettes garnish); fold into custard. Pour mixture into pie shell and chill. Garnish with rosettes of whipped cream and chocolate shavings before serving.

Note: packaged custard mix may be used and liqueur substituted for about one quarter of the required liquid.

Serves 8 to 10

Avocado Kiwi Cream Liqueur Refrigerator Pie

 1 prepared, 9-inch graham cracker crust or our
   homemade crust omitting sugar (page 90)
 3 medium-size ripe avocados
 ¼ cup lemon juice
 1 can (14 ounces) sweetened condensed milk
 ¼ cup *kiwi cream liqueur* (page 46)
 3 kiwifruit, sliced thin
 Non-dairy whipped topping
 Chopped walnuts

Prepare filling. Peel avocados and remove pits. Combine avocados, lemon juice, condensed milk, and kiwi liqueur in food processor or blender. Blend 3 to 5 minutes or until smooth.

Assemble pie. Peel and slice kiwifruit. Use slices from two kiwifruits and layer on bottom of piecrust. Pour avocado mixture into crust and cover top completely with whipped topping. Sprinkle with walnuts and peeled, sliced kiwifruit. Chill in refrigerator 3 hours and serve.

Serves 8 to 10

Individual Strawberry Butterfly Shell Tarts

1 package prepared ready-to-bake piecrust
1½ pints fresh strawberries, hulled
1 cup sugar
3 tablespoons cornstarch
½ cup water
1 package (3 ounces) cream cheese, softened
½ cup *strawberry cream liqueur* (page 48)

Prepare crust. Bake pie crust according to package directions for single-shell pies. Cool. Cut into 8 slices and place two in each dessert dish with one slice on each side of dish.

Prepare filling and glaze. Set aside 8 whole berries. Crush 1 cup of strawberries and slice 1 cup. Prepare glaze by mixing sugar and cornstarch together in saucepan and gradually stirring in water and crushed strawberries. Cook over medium heat, stirring constantly until mixture thickens and boils. Boil and stir 1 minute. Cool.

Assemble tarts. Beat cream cheese until smooth. Spread at bottom of baked pie crust pieces. Spread a coating of *strawberry cream liqueur* over cheese. Fill shell with sliced berries. Pour glaze over berries. Garnish with whole berries. Pour *strawberry cream liqueur* over top and serve extra in a small cream pitcher.
Serves 4

Easy, Elegant, Banana Cream Liqueur Custard Pie

      1 prepared, 9-inch piecrust or use our piecrust recipe
          (page 90)
      1 package (5 ounces) banana cream instant pudding
          and pie filling
      2½ cups cold milk
      ½ cup cold *banana cream liqueur* (page 44)
      2 ripe bananas
      1 cup whipping cream
      ¼ cup *banana cream liqueur* (page 44)
      Slivered, toasted almonds

Prepare crust. Bake piecrust according to directions for single-crust pie. Cool. Slice bananas and arrange in a single layer on baked piecrust.

Prepare filling. Prepare instant pudding mix according to directions, but using a mixture of 2½ cups cold milk with ½ cup cold *banana cream liqueur.*

Assemble pie. Pour into piecrust and refrigerate at least 1 hour. Whip cream, adding ¼ cup *banana cream liqueur.* Mound onto pie. Use a pastry bag to make whipped cream swirls. Decorate with slivered almonds.

Serves 8

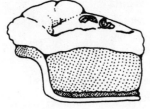

Cream Puffs

Cream puff shells may be filled with any flavored whipped cream, custard, pudding, or pastry cream filling. We offer recipes for two whipped cream fillings: cappuccino-espresso and vanilla. However, if you mix the whipped cream and chocolate glaze with any flavor liqueur you have on hand, it will work as well.

Puff shells:
½ cup butter cut into small pieces
1 cup water
Pinch of salt
1 tablespoon sugar
1 cup all-purpose flour, sifted
5 eggs at room temperature

Cappuccino-espresso filling:
1 cup whipping cream
2 tablespoons cocoa powder
1 tablespoon instant cappuccino coffee espresso powder
¼ cup *mocha chocolate cream liqueur* (page 41)

Alternate filling—vanilla cream:
1 cup whipping cream
½ teaspoon pure vanilla
¼ cup *vanilla cream liqueur* (page 42)
Food coloring (optional)

Chocolate sauce:
6 ounces semisweet chocolate broken into small pieces
½ cup whipping cream
1 teaspoon cream liqueur (same flavor used in cream
    filling)

Prepare puff shells. Preheat oven to 400° F. Heat butter, water, salt, and sugar in a small saucepan until butter melts and liquid begins to boil. Remove from heat. Add flour all at once and beat with wooden spoon until mixed. Place pan over medium heat and continue to beat until mixture pulls away from sides of pan and does not stick to spoon. Remove from heat and cool 3 minutes. Add eggs one at a time, beating vigorously with the wooden spoon after each addition until the dough is smooth and no longer looks slippery. Test for readiness by lifting a peak of dough with the spoon tip. If it stands upright, it is done.

Use a spoon or pastry bag with a ¾-inch plain tip. Spoon or pipe 3-inch circles of dough onto a lightly greased baking sheet, leaving space between them for expansion. Bake 35 to 40 minutes or until puffed and golden. Cool away from drafts. Cut off tops and remove any filaments of soft dough from the inside.

Prepare filling. Beat whipping cream in small bowl until it begins to hold shape. Add sugar, coffee and cocoa powders, and continue to beat until soft peaks form. Fold in liqueur. (Cream may be colored with a drop of food coloring.) Pipe or spoon filling into shells. Place top of shell on filling.

Prepare sauce. Melt chocolate with cream and liqueur in double boiler over gently simmering water. Stir until smooth. Spoon over top of puff shell.

Makes 12

Chocolate Rum Mousse

This recipe can be served in a glass or as a pie or pastry filling.

¼ cup sugar
3 tablespoons rum
4 ounces semisweet or sweet chocolate
3 tablespoons whipping cream
4 tablespoons *chocolate cream liqueur* (use a rum base)
    (page 57)
2 egg whites
2 cups whipped cream

Cook sugar with rum in saucepan over low heat just until sugar is dissolved and achieves the consistency of syrup. Melt chocolate and stir in whipping cream and liqueur. Add rum/sugar syrup to chocolate and stir until smooth. Cool, but do not chill. Fold two stiffly beaten egg whites into cooled chocolate. Then, stir this mixture into 2 cups whipped cream.

Spoon into sherbet glasses or favorite pastry shell (see Chapter 6). Chill 2 hours before serving.

Serves 8 to 10

Your Favorite Flavor Fruit Pie

This is a quick-to-whip-up pie that uses what you have available. Use in-season fruits or canned fruits, and any flavor of cream liqueur you like. Make it in less than 8 minutes. Ready to eat after chilling about 3 hours.

8- or 9-inch homemade graham cracker or other crumb crust (pages 89–90)
1 package (3 ounces) gelatin, any flavor
⅔ cup boiling water
2 cups ice cubes
3½ cups or one 8-ounce container non-dairy whipped topping
¼ cup cream liqueur compatible in flavor to fruit
1 cup diced fresh fruit or canned, drained fruit

Prepare filling. Dissolve gelatin in hot water by stirring about 3 minutes. Add ice cubes and stir until gelatin thickens in 2 to 3 minutes. Remove any unmelted ice. Blend in whipped topping and liqueur with wire whip, until smooth. Fold in fruit.

Assemble pie. Spoon into piecrust. Chill about 3 hours. Garnish top with sliced fruit or additional whipped topping if desired.

Serves 8

FRUITS WITH CREAM LIQUEURS

Pears in Creamy Mocha Sauce

8 fresh pears
Lemon juice
¼ cup sugar
1 cup water
½ cup *mocha chocolate cream liqueur* (page 41)
5 ounces semisweet chocolate
2 tablespoons butter

Peel pears and leave them whole without removing center. Brush with lemon juice to preserve color. Combine sugar and water in medium-size saucepan over low heat. When sugar is dissolved, add pears, cover and simmer 25 minutes or until pears are tender but firm. Remove pears from syrup with slotted spoon and arrange on serving dish. Refrigerate.

Boil remaining syrup until about ¼ cup remains. Add liqueur and boil until about ⅔ cup remains. Add chocolate, stirring constantly until sauce is smooth. Beat in butter a little at a time. Chill. Pour sauce over pears just before serving.

Serves 8

Flavored Fruit Yogurt Delights

This filling may be placed in a piecrust or in individual serving glasses. Use a flavored yogurt with fruits in season and add your choice of cream liqueur and additional fresh fruit. We offer it with banana-peach but try your favorite flavor combinations.

Crumb crust (pages 89–90)
½ cup *banana cream liqueur* (page 44)
2 containers peach yogurt
1 container (8 or 9 ounces) non-dairy topping
1 cup cut-up fresh peaches

Press crumb crust in bottom and slightly up sides of 8 champagne glasses or dessert dishes. Mix liqueur into yogurt. Fold yogurt into topping. Spoon into glasses or pastry shell. Garnish with extra fruit slices or other decoration.

Serves 8

New England Orange Cream Cobbler

Filling:
4 cups fresh, sliced peaches or 4 cups drained, sliced
    peaches
½ cup *peach cream liqueur* (page 47)
¼ cup sugar
½ teaspoon cinnamon

Topping:
2 eggs
1 cup flour
1 cup sugar
1 teaspoon baking soda
½ teaspoon salt
4 tablespoons butter, softened
2 tablespoons *orange cream liqueur* (page 47)

Garnish:
Whipping cream (or ice cream)
1 tablespoon *peach cream liqueur* (page 47)
1 tablespoon *orange cream liqueur* (page 47)

Preheat oven to 375°F. Place peach slices in an 8-inch baking dish at least 2 inches deep. Sprinkle with mixture of sugar and cinnamon and *orange cream liqueur*. Beat eggs, add sugar and flour mixed with baking soda and salt. Beat with mixer on low speed until blended. Add butter and blend thoroughly. Drop by teaspoonfuls on top of peaches in baking dish. Bake about 45 minutes. Whip cream and add liqueurs (or ice cream with liqueurs added). Cobbler may be served warm or cold with whipped cream.
Serves 6 to 8

Sliced Apples with Chocolate Cream Liqueur

3 large Granny Smith or other baking apples
¼ cup butter or margarine
2 tablespoons brown sugar
½ cup *chocolate mint cream liqueur* (page 51)
1 teaspoon cinnamon
1 teaspoon nutmeg
½ cup raisins
1 cup non-dairy whipped topping
2 tablespoons *chocolate mint cream liqueur* (page 51)

Preheat oven to 350°F. Arrange sliced apples in flan or quiche dish. Drizzle with dabs of butter or margarine. Sprinkle with brown sugar and ½ cup liqueur. Add cinnamon, nutmeg, and raisins. Cover with aluminum foil. Bake 30 minutes or until apples are soft. Serve warm. Mix topping with 2 tablespoons liqueur and drop by tablespoons over apples. Sprinkle with cinnamon.
Serves 6 to 8

7 Cookies and Cupcakes

A hint of liqueur flavor in cookie dough or in fillings and frostings can make even the simplest cookie recipe taste special. A dash of spirit will perk up cupcakes and muffins, too. If you are adding dried fruits, such as raisins or apricot pieces, plump them up by letting them soak in the liqueur for about 15 minutes.

Cookies are made in many ways: by dropping them on cookie sheets, pushing dough through a cookie press, or cutting from dough. Then, there are squares and bars.

We offer recipes for many varieties. The consistency of dough may vary with size of eggs and your altitude. In altitudes over 5,000 feet, cookies rich in chocolate may require a reduction of about one half of the baking powder or soda.

Always bake cookies in a preheated oven.

Cupcakes and muffin recipes also are offered in this chapter. They demonstrate that you can improvise recipes and add cream liqueurs; it's a trick you can catch on to quickly, especially when using packaged mixes.

The liqueurs used in the recipes in this chapter that are italicized are homemade recipes given in Chapter 3. Another flavor or a commercial cream liqueur may be substituted.

COOKIES

Butterscotch Coconut Cookie Bars

½ cup butter or margarine
1½ cups graham cracker crumbs
1 cup (14-ounce can) sweetened condensed milk
¾ cup *coconut cream liqueur* (page 58, make your own
     clear liqueur, then add cream)
2 cups (12-ounce package) butterscotch chips
1⅓ cups flaked coconut
1 cup chopped walnuts
½ cup raisins (optional)

Preheat oven to 350°F (325°F for glass pans). Place butter in 13" × 9" baking pan and put in oven to melt. Sprinkle graham cracker crumbs over butter. Pour sweetened condensed milk and then liqueur evenly over crumbs. Top with remaining ingredients in even layers. Press down with palm of hand. Bake 25 to 30 minutes or until lightly browned. Cool. Refrigerate. Cut into bars. These freeze well.

Makes 36 bars

Nutty Cheese-Filled Almond Cookies

1 cup (½ pound) butter or margarine, softened
½ cup firmly packed brown sugar
2 eggs separated
½ teaspoon pure vanilla extract
¼ cup *amaretto cream liqueur* (page 37)
2½ cups all-purpose flour
¼ teaspoon salt
2 cups finely chopped walnuts
4 ounces cream cheese softened
3 tablespoons *amaretto cream liqueur* (page 37)

Preheat oven to 375°F. Grease baking sheet. Cream butter and sugar in large bowl with electric mixer. Beat yolks and vanilla into butter mixture. Blend in ¼ cup liqueur. In a small bowl, lightly beat egg whites and set aside. Stir flour and salt together. Gradually add to butter mixture and blend thoroughly.

Shape cookies into balls 1 inch in diameter. Roll each ball in egg white, then in finely chopped walnuts to coat. Place on baking sheet, spacing 1 inch apart. Indent the center of each cookie with your thumb or the tip of a teaspoon. Mix cream cheese with 3 tablespoons liqueur. Neatly fill each indentation with about ¼ teaspoon of the cheese mixture. Bake 12 to 15 minutes or until lightly browned. Cool on baking sheet about 1 minute, then loosen with spatula and let cool. Store in airtight canister.

Makes about 48 cookies

Cassis Rum Oatmeal Cookies

1 cup raisins
½ cup *crème de cassis cream liqueur* (page 51)
¾ cup shortening, softened
1 cup brown sugar
½ cup sugar
1 egg
¼ cup water
1 tablespoon *crème de cassis cream liqueur* (page 51)
1 cup sifted flour
1 teaspoon salt
½ teaspoon baking soda
3 cups quick oats
Chocolate chips, nuts, chopped dates (optional)

Preheat oven to 350°F. Grease cookie sheet. Plump raisins in hot water about 10 minutes. Drain and pat dry on paper towel. Pour ½ cup *crème de cassis cream liqueur* over raisins and let soak while you prepare batter. In a large bowl, mix shortening, sugars, egg, water, and liqueur and beat thoroughly. In another bowl, sift together flour, salt, and soda. Add gradually to shortening mixture and blend well. Mix in oats. Drain raisins and fold into mixture. (Add optional nuts, etc.) Drop by teaspoons about 1 inch apart onto cookie sheet. Bake 12 to 15 minutes or until golden brown.
Makes approximately 48 cookies

Rocky Road Mint Cookies

  1 cup (14-ounce can) sweetened condensed milk
  1 cup (6 ounces) semisweet chocolate chips
  1 cup (6 ounces) chocolate mint squares broken into
      pieces the size of chips
  ¼ cup *Kahlùa-mint Irish cream liqueur* (page 50)
  1 cup chopped walnuts or peanuts
  2½ cups miniature marshmallows

Butter generously a 9-inch square pan. Combine milk and all chips in a 2-quart saucepan. Cook over low heat, stirring constantly until chocolate is melted. Stir in liqueur. Stir in nuts, then 1½ cups of the marshmallows. Sprinkle remaining marshmallows over bottom of pan. Spoon chocolate mixture over marshmallows, spreading carefully. Refrigerate 2 hours or until firm. Cut into pieces with sharp knife.
Makes approximately 48 pieces

Chocolate-Dipped Store-Bought Cookies

  2 cups (12-ounce package) semisweet chocolate chips
  3 tablespoons vegetable oil
  1 tablespoon any flavor cream liqueur (see Chapter 3
      for ideas)
  Store-bought cookies such as chocolate and vanilla
      sandwich cookies, vanilla wafers, pretzels, or fig
      bars

Melt chocolate (see pages 79–80 for proper method), add oil a little at a time, and add liqueur. Dip cookies in chocolate and place on waxed paper.
Dipping for about 5 dozen cookies

Chocolate-Covered Praline Cookies

1½ cups flour
1½ teaspoons baking powder
½ teaspoon salt
1½ cups brown sugar, packed
⅔ cup shortening
1 egg
2 tablespoons *amaretto cream liqueur* (page 37)
½ cup chopped pecans

Dipping chocolate:
2 cups (12-ounce package) semisweet chocolate pieces
3 tablespoons oil
1 tablespoon *amaretto cream liqueur* (page 37)

Preheat oven to 350°F. Grease baking sheet. Combine flour, baking powder, salt, brown sugar, shortening, egg, liqueur, and pecans. Roll into ½-inch balls and place on baking sheet. Bake 10 to 12 minutes. Cool. Melt chocolate for dipping, stir in oil a little at a time, and add liqueur. Hold cookie with tongs and dip into chocolate to cover only half of cookie.
Makes about 5 dozen cookies

Chocolate Wafer Cream Sandwiches

8 ounces non-dairy topping
2 tablespoons any flavor cream liqueur (see Chapter 3)
1 package chocolate wafer cookies (or other thin cookie)
Walnut halves or cake-decorating sprinkles

Mix liqueur into topping and spread on one cookie and top with another to make sandwiches. Add dollop of topping on top cookie. Decorate with walnut half or sprinkles. May be made as single cookies (not sandwiches) by adding topping only.
Makes 2 to 4 dozen cookies

Greek Amaretto Butter Cookies (Kourabiethes)

1 pound sweet butter, softened
½ cup sugar
2 egg yolks
½ teaspoon pure vanilla extract
4½ cups all-purpose flour
1 teaspoon baking powder
¼ teaspoon ground cloves
1 cup almonds, chopped
1 tablespoon *amaretto cream liqueur* (page 37)
1 cup powdered sugar

Preheat oven to 375°F. Soften butter to room temperature and beat with electric mixer until butter turns white (about 10 minutes). Add sugar, egg yolks, and vanilla, beat thoroughly. Sift together flour, baking powder, and cloves. Add to butter mixture. Mix well. Stir in chopped almonds. Sprinkle dough with liqueur and knead until it holds together. Shape into crescents and place on ungreased cookie sheet 1 inch apart. Bake for 15 to 20 minutes or until lightly browned. Roll cookies in powdered sugar.
Makes about 6 dozen cookies

CUPCAKES

Add two or three teaspoons of cream liqueur to the batter of your favorite dessert cupcakes. For a different touch, add a dollop of filling mixed with cream liqueur to each cupcake. Try 4 ounces of cream cheese, softened and mixed with 2 to 3 tablespoons of liqueur. Fill muffin cup to one-third, add the cheese, and add another spoonful of batter. The cheese creates a subtle, filled center. Mix liqueurs into custard fillings, too. Add them to icings and soft buttercream frostings.

Mocha Liqueur Black Bottom Cupcakes

Mixture 1:
6 ounces cream cheese
2 eggs, beaten
2 tablespoons *coffee cream liqueur* (page 56)
¼ teaspoon salt
½ cup sugar
2 cups (12-ounce package) chocolate chips

Mixture 2:
3 cups all-purpose flour
½ cup cocoa
2 teaspoons baking soda
2 cups sugar
1 teaspoon salt
2 cups water
⅔ cup cooking oil
2 tablespoons vinegar
2 teaspoons *coffee cream liqueur* (page 56)

Preheat oven to 350°F. Beat together cheese, eggs, liqueur, salt, and sugar until smooth. Stir in chocolate chips. Set aside. Sift together flour, cocoa, baking soda, sugar, and salt. Add water, oil, vinegar, and liqueur. Beat well. Place 36 large paper or foil cupcake liners in muffin or cupcake tins. Fill each with mixture 2, slightly more than half. Drop one teaspoon of mixture 1 on top of each. Bake 25 minutes.

Makes 36 cupcakes

Oat Bran Muffins with Banana
Cream Cheese Filling

2 eggs
½ cup oil
1 cup buttermilk
⅓ cup honey
⅓ cup molasses
2 cups oat bran
1⅔ cups whole wheat flour
¼ cup brown sugar
2½ teaspoons baking soda
½ cup raisins
6 ounces cream cheese
½ cup *banana cream liqueur* (page 44)

Preheat oven to 400°F. Grease muffin tin cups or use paper or foil liners. Beat eggs lightly in bowl. Stir in oil, buttermilk, honey, and molasses. Stir together bran, flour, brown sugar, baking soda, and raisins in large mixing bowl. Add egg mixture to flour mixture and stir just until all ingredients are blended.

In a small bowl, whip cream cheese and liqueur to use as filling. Fill muffin cups with batter about one-half full. Drop a heaping tablespoon of cream cheese filling into each muffin cup. Put more muffin batter over cream cheese until cups are three-quarters full. Bake 12 to 15 minutes or until wood toothpick inserted in center of muffin comes out clean.
Makes 20 to 24 muffins

Cupcakes with Pudding Centers

1 package prepared cupcake mix with pudding filling
¼ to ½ cup cream liqueur (any flavor; see Chapter 3)

Mix cupcakes according to package directions. Mix pudding filling, but substitute one half of the liquid called for with cream liqueur. Bake as directed.
Makes approximately 12 cupcakes

8 Candies and Confections

If one could physically taste elegance, one would choose to eat a liqueured candy. Liqueur flavored and filled candies cannot be made commercially in most of the United States. If you see them in a candy store, they probably were shipped from Nevada, where such candy making is legal. But, there's nothing to stop you from making them at home for your own consumption. (Just don't try to market them at your club's next bazaar!)

We've selected easy-to-make recipes that require no previous candy-making experience. You can make most of them without a candy thermometer or molds in about a half hour or so. Watch for other easy candy recipes on the backs of cereal boxes, cans of sweetened condensed milk, and on labels and packages from baking chocolate and chocolate chips. Improvise your own recipes and flavor combinations by adding a tablespoon or two of your homemade cream liqueur to the chocolate or to the sweetened condensed milk called for in the recipe.

A few general hints about candy making: use unsalted butter when butter is called for and avoid making candy on hot, humid days. Chocolate may behave unpredictably. See pages 79–80 for chocolate melting procedures over stove and in microwave oven.

The liqueurs used in the recipes in this chapter that are italicized are homemade recipes given in Chapter 3. Another flavor or a commercial cream liqueur may be substituted.

Orange Chocolate Truffles

> 6 ounces (6 squares) semisweet chocolate cut or broken into small pieces
> ½ cup unsalted butter
> 2 tablespoons heavy cream
> 4 tablespoons *orange cream liqueur* (page 47)
> 1 cup sifted powdered sugar
> ¼ cup grated walnuts (or pecans or hazelnuts)
> ¼ cup cocoa powder
> ¼ cup Irish whiskey instant coffee powder

Melt chocolate with butter. Stir, adding cream gradually. Remove from heat and stir in *triple sec cream liqueur*. Gradually stir in sugar until free of lumps. Stir in nuts. Let mixture stand covered in a cool place 12 to 24 hours. Mix cocoa powder and instant coffee on waxed paper and place some on palms of hands so chocolate won't stick as you roll it. Scoop chocolate with teaspoon and quickly shape into a small ball for each truffle and roll each ball in cocoa/coffee powder mixed in a small, flat dish. Place on waxed paper on cookie sheet. Refrigerate immediately.

Makes about 4 dozen truffles

Cognac Cream Balls

> 2 tablespoons cocoa
> 1 cup powdered sugar
> ¼ cup *cognac-base cream liqueur* (page 39) or Häagen-
>   Dazs cream liqueur
> 2 tablespoons light corn syrup
> 2½ cups crushed vanilla wafers
> 1 cup broken nuts (pecans, walnuts, almonds, etc.)
> ½ cup powdered sugar

Sift together cocoa and powdered sugar. Combine liqueur and corn syrup and stir into cocoa mix. Add syrup, wafers, and nuts and mix thoroughly. Roll mixture into small balls and dredge in powdered sugar.

Makes about 24 candies

Coconut Rum Pecan Fudge

> 1 cup pecans
> ¼ cup unsalted butter
> 1 cup brown sugar, packed
> 1 cup sugar
> 2 teaspoons mocha instant coffee powder
> ¼ teaspoon salt
> ¼ cup *mocha coconut rum cream liqueur* (page 42)
> ⅝ cup sour cream

Chop ½ cup of the pecans into medium-fine pieces for main recipe. Chop other ½ cup into fine pieces for coating fudge. Melt butter in 2-quart saucepan. Add sugars, instant coffee, and salt. Stir liqueur into sour cream and add to pan. Cook over low heat, stirring until sugars dissolve. Cover. Boil slowly 4 to 5 minutes. Then uncover and cook rapidly without stirring to 236°F (to form soft ball). Remove from heat. Cool to lukewarm. Add vanilla. Beat until mixture is creamy and begins to hold its shape. Gently fold in medium-size pecan pieces. Drop rounded teaspoonfuls onto waxed paper. Quickly shape into balls. Roll in finely chopped pecans. Let stand or refrigerate to harden.

Makes 24 candies

Chocolate-Dipped Strawberries

>   18 large, fresh strawberries washed and placed on a
>   paper towel to dry
>   2 cups (12-ounce package) semisweet chocolate chips
>   1 tablespoon solid shortening
>   1 tablespoon *strawberry cream liqueur* (page 48)
>   2 cups (12 ounces) white chocolate, cut into small
>   pieces
>   1 to 1½ tablespoons solid shortening
>   1 tablespoon *coconut cappuccino cream liqueur* (page 38)

Melt semisweet chocolate with 1 tablespoon shortening in double boiler. Add *strawberry cream liqueur* and stir until smooth. Remove from heat, but keep over hot water. Tilt pan to keep pool of chocolate deep. Dip ¾ of the strawberry in chocolate to coat it. Set on waxed paper on tray and chill just to firm chocolate.

Melt white chocolate as above, with shortening. Add *coconut cappuccino cream liqueur*. You may need to add an extra ½ tablespoon shortening to white chocolate to achieve dipping consistency. For a white drizzle effect on dark chocolate (not shown), remove dark chocolate strawberries from refrigerator; dip fork tines in melted white chocolate and, holding strawberry over pan, drizzle white chocolate over dark chocolate in a quick steady motion as you turn the berry to achieve a striped or swirled effect.

The same result can be achieved with peeled orange segments or apple slices. Chill until firm and cover loosely with plastic wrap. Or melt white chocolate and dip strawberries as above.

Chunky Chocolate Banana Coconut Cubes

⅓ cup vegetable oil
2 squares (1 ounce each) semisweet or unsweetened
    chocolate
1¼ cups unsifted all-purpose flour
¾ cup sugar
½ cup water
1 egg
½ cup *banana coconut rum cream liqueur* (page 44)
½ teaspoon salt
½ teaspoon baking soda
½ teaspoon pure vanilla extract
⅔ cup flaked coconut
6 squares (1 ounce each) semisweet chocolate, chopped
½ cup chopped nuts (optional)

Heat oil and 2 squares chocolate in 8-inch square pan in 350°F
oven until melted. Add flour, sugar, water, egg, liqueur, salt, baking
soda, and vanilla; blend with fork until smooth. Stir in coconut.
Sprinkle with chopped chocolate and nuts if desired. Bake at 350°F
for 40 minutes. Cool in pan. Cut into 1-inch, candy-size squares and
place each in a paper candy cup.
Makes 56 squares

Chocolate Orange Raisin-Nut Clusters

> 8 squares (½ pound) semisweet chocolate
> 2 tablespoons solid shortening
> ¾ cup sweetened condensed milk
> 2 tablespoons *orange-chocolate cream liqueur* (page 42)
> ½ cup nuts broken into pieces (walnuts, pecans,
>   hazelnuts, or unsalted peanuts)
> ⅔ cup raisins (dark, golden, or mixed)

Place chocolate in large measuring cup or pan and heat until melted. Stir in shortening and let melt. Stir milk in slowly, then add liqueur until well-blended. Add nuts and raisins. Drop candy from a teaspoon onto waxed paper to make about a ¾ inch circle. Let stand or refrigerate to cool.
Makes about 36 clusters

Cherry Chocolate Rocky Road Candy

> 6 ounces (6 squares) semisweet chocolate
> 1 square unsweetened chocolate
> 1 tablespoon unsalted butter
> 1 egg
> 2 tablespoons *cherry cream liqueur* (page 45)
> 1½ cups powdered sugar
> ½ teaspoon salt
> 1 teaspoon pure vanilla extract
> 2 cups unsalted peanuts
> 2 cups miniature marshmallows

Melt chocolate and butter in large bowl in microwave (or large pan on stove, stirring until smooth). Let cool as you prepare egg mixture. In another bowl, beat egg until foamy. Mix in liqueur, sugar, salt, and vanilla. Blend in chocolate mixture. Stir in peanuts and marshmallows. Drop by teaspoonfuls onto waxed paper. Chill until firm (about 2 hours). Store in refrigerator.
Makes about 4 dozen candies

Coconut Cappuccino Caramel Turtles

½ pound soft caramels
3 tablespoons *coconut cappuccino cream liqueur* (page 38)
1 cup pecan halves
4 ounces (4 squares) semisweet chocolate
4 tablespoons flaked coconut

Melt caramels with liqueur in saucepan over very low heat, stirring constantly. Cool 10 minutes. Lightly butter a baking sheet. Place five pecans in cluster with one in center for turtle body and four overlapping center and extending for "feet." Spoon caramel over nuts to hold together but leave tips of feet showing. Let stand to cool and set. Melt chocolate and spread over caramel mixture. Sprinkle coconut on melted chocolate. Cool to set.

Makes about 20 candies

9 Sauces, Quiches, Fondue, and Flan

Cream liqueurs may be stirred into sauces that usually have fruits or milk and cream as their base. You can pour liqueurs over stewed and fresh fruits, ice creams, puddings, pies, and pound cakes. Marinate fresh fruits for several hours in the liqueur, then drain. We've provided unusual flavorings using a variety of ingredients. Be inventive and combine flavors. A blackberry cream brandy based liqueur may be delicious mixed with fresh raspberries. You'll find recipes for liqueur-loaded quiches, fondues, flan, and gelatin molds, too.

Surprise your diners with these recipes—they provide off-beat tastes for new gourmet experiences. You'll be glad you did.

The liqueurs used in the recipes in this chapter that are italicized are homemade recipes given in Chapter 3. Another flavor or a commercial cream liqueur may be substituted.

SAUCES

Irish Cream Sauce

> 1 cup sugar
> 2½ tablespoons cornstarch
> ½ teaspoon salt
> ¼ teaspoon ground cinnamon
> 3 cups water
> 2 tablespoons *Irish cream liqueur* (page 40)

Combine dry ingredients in a saucepan. Gradually stir in water and liqueur. Bring to boil over medium heat, stirring constantly. Simmer 5 minutes. Serve over fruit desserts or over ice cream.
Makes 3 cups

Strawberry Cream Sauce

> ¾ cup strawberry preserves
> ¼ cup *strawberry cream liqueur* (page 47)

Blend preserves and liqueur. Serve over puddings, baked fruits, and ice creams. Try this with any flavor preserves and a compatible flavor cream liqueur. It's probably the quickest, most exceptional sauce you can make.
Makes about 1 cup

Fresh Blueberry Sauce

> 3 cups fresh blueberries, rinsed and drained
> ⅓ cup superfine sugar
> 3 tablespoons *berry cream liqueur* (page 45, use
>   blueberries)

Puree blueberries in blender or food processor until smooth. Stir sugar into puree until dissolved. Stir in liqueur. Delicious served over other fruits, puddings, or ice cream. May be stored in glass jar in refrigerator 3 to 4 days, or put in freezer.
Makes about 2 cups

Chantilly Cream

⅔ cup heavy cream
1 teaspoon pure vanilla extract
2 teaspoons *orange cream liqueur* (page 47)
¼ cup sugar
2 tablespoons sour cream

Chill a medium-size bowl and beaters in freezer for about a half hour. Combine cream, vanilla, and liqueur in bowl and beat with electric mixer on medium speed for 1 minute. Add sugar and sour cream. Beat on medium until soft peaks form, for about 3 minutes. Do not overbeat. A marvelous sauce over bread, cakes, or rice puddings.
Makes about 1 cup

Mocha Coconut Cappuccino Fudge Sauce

1 cup brown sugar, packed
1 tablespoon coffee-flavored instant powder
¼ cup *coconut cappuccino cream liqueur* (page 38)
2 tablespoons light corn syrup
2 tablespoons butter
1 teaspoon pure vanilla extract

Combine all ingredients in a saucepan except vanilla. Bring to a boil, stirring until sugar dissolves. Simmer and stir about 4 minutes. Add vanilla. Serve over cream puffs, ice cream, or other pastry.
Makes about 1½ cups

Peach Cream Sauce

½ cup sugar
1½ tablespoons cornstarch
¼ teaspoon salt
2 cups boiling water
1 tablespoon pure vanilla extract
¼ cup *peach cream liqueur* (page 47)

Combine sugar, cornstarch, and salt in saucepan. Mix well. Add boiling water slowly while stirring. Put pan on heat, bring to boil, and continue slow boiling for 4 to 5 minutes. Add vanilla and liqueur. Chill. This sauce is good with fresh mango.
Makes about 2½ cups

QUICHE—QUICK, QUIVERY, QUALITY

Mocha Chocolate Quiche

Follow above recipe for crust, omitting almonds.

Filling:
18 ounces semisweet chocolate
7 egg yolks
1¼ cups heavy cream
½ cup *mocha-chocolate cream liqueur* (page 41)

Garnish (optional):
Whipped cream
Shaved chocolate

Preheat oven to 375°F. Prepare crust and line quiche pan. Heat chocolate in saucepan to melt. Remove from heat and cool slightly. In another bowl, beat together egg yolks and cream until well-blended. Add the liqueur and blend. Add the melted chocolate and mix well. Pour into crust. Place pan on cookie sheet and bake about 45 minutes or until top appears firm. Let cool completely. May be served with whipped cream and shaved chocolate.
Serves 8

Blueberry Quiche Amaretto

Almond crust:
¾ cup sifted all-purpose flour
¼ teaspoon salt
½ cup ground almonds, blanched or raw, or almond meal
⅓ cup shortening
2 tablespoons firm butter
3 tablespoons cold milk
(You may use a packaged dough, or ready-made piecrust)

Filling:
½ pound (8-ounce package) cream cheese
2 teaspoons sugar
¼ teaspoon salt
⅛ teaspoon cinnamon
4 large eggs
½ cup *amaretto cream liqueur* (page 37)
1¼ cups thin cream (half and half)
1 pint fresh blueberries (or other berries in season),
    washed and patted dry

Prepare crust. Combine flour, salt, and ground almonds in a bowl. Cut the shortening and butter into flour with a pastry cutter or break up with fingertips until dough is crumbly. Add just enough milk to make dough stiff. Shape into ball. Roll out on floured board to a 13-inch circle. Gently fit into an 11-inch diameter quiche pan, lining bottom and sides. Turn edge in and shape a rim about ⅛ inch above pan edge. Chill one hour.

Prepare filling. Set oven rack below oven center. Preheat oven to 375° F. Have all filling ingredients at room temperature. Beat cream cheese with sugar, salt, and cinnamon in a small bowl until soft. Beat in one egg at a time. Add *amaretto cream liqueur* until mixture is smooth. Stir in half and half.

Assemble quiche. Carefully pour filling into chilled crust. Set filled pan on a cookie sheet and place both in oven. Bake until filling is barely set in center and golden brown on top (about 45 minutes). Cool on wire rack. Serve with remaining blueberries and other fruit in season.

Serves 8

FONDUES

The word *fondue* originally applied to cheese sauces from Switzerland, according to *The New Larousse Gastronomique*. But contemporary chefs have used the idea of a hot, delicious sauce as the basis for a variety of recipes with diverse ingredients. Among their creations are marvelous chocolate fondues into which you may dip fruits, pieces of cake, cookies, and so forth.

White Chocolate Fondue

> 12 ounces white chocolate, grated
> ⅔ cup *vanilla cream liqueur* (page 42)

Melt white chocolate in saucepan over low heat or in microwave. Remove from heat, add *vanilla cream liqueur* gradually until chocolate is a dipping consistency. Keep warm in fondue pan. Fruit to be dipped should be patted dry. Use strawberries, apple slices, pineapple slices, or orange sections. Also dip cookies or pretzels.

FLAN AND CUSTARD

Orange Liqueur–Flavored Flan

1¾ cups sugar
3 egg whites
8 egg yolks
2 cans evaporated milk (13-ounce size)
1 teaspoon pure vanilla extract
2 teaspoons *orange cream liqueur* (page 47) or triple sec
   or Grand Marnier

Prepare caramel sauce. Place 1 cup sugar in small, non-stick saucepan, heat on low, and stir constantly until sugar melts and turns to a golden syrup. Pour enough to cover only the bottom of each of 8 individual custard cups or one 9-inch flan pan. Quickly tip dishes so caramel covers bottom and sides. Cool.

Prepare custard. Preheat oven to 350° F. Beat egg whites and yolks together, then add milk, remaining sugar, vanilla, and liqueur, mixing well. Strain into coated dishes. Cover with foil and place dishes in a larger pan containing hot water that reaches about halfway up side of custard cups or flan pan. Bake about 1 hour or until a knife inserted in center comes out clean. Cool, but while still warm invert container to unmold. If it is too cool, caramel will stick to dishes. Chill thoroughly.

Note: Commercial flan mix may be used and liqueur added when mixing.

Serves 8

GELATIN MOLDS

Any recipe for molded gelatin that calls for cream cheese, cream, or milk for a creamy opaque appearance can accept a cream liqueur. Use liqueur with fruit fillings and with vegetable gelatins and aspic recipes, too.

Creamy Orange Mango Carrot Mold

> 1 package (6-ounce size or two 3-ounce packages)
>   orange-flavored gelatin
> 2 cups boiling water
> 1 cup cold water
> ½ cup *mango cream liqueur* (page 46)
> 3 oranges, peeled and sectioned
> ½ cup shredded carrots
> Lettuce leaves
> Carrot curls

Dissolve gelatin in boiling water. Add cold water and liqueur. Pour ¾ cup of the mixture into a 6-cup mold. Chill until set but not firm. Arrange 12 to 15 orange sections overlapped in a layer in mold. Add another ½ cup gelatin mixture over oranges. Chill until set but not firm and chill remaining gelatin until thickened. Dice remaining orange sections. Fold oranges and shredded carrots into thickened gelatin. Spoon into mold. Chill at least 4 hours until firm. Unmold and serve on a bed of washed, dried lettuce, garnish with carrot curls and additional orange slices, if desired. Or, serve a pitcher of liqueur as a sauce.

Serves 8 to 10

Fruit-Nut Gelatin Mold with Cream Liqueur

1 package fruit-flavored gelatin (3-ounce size)
1¾ cup boiling water
¼ cup fruit- or nut-flavored cream liqueur (see
    Chapter 3)
½ cup chopped fruit
¼ cup chopped nuts

Dissolve gelatin in boiling water. Cool slightly. Add liqueur and then stir in fruit and nuts. Pour into greased mold or bowl. Refrigerate until firm. Unmold on platter. Serve with pitcher of liqueur as a sauce, if desired.
Serves 4

Appendix

EQUIVALENTS— CONVERSION MEASURES

The following lists offer equivalents to liquid and dry measures as well as weight to simplify conversions. U.S., British, and metric equivalents are given.

U.S. Liquid Measure Volume Equivalents

A pinch =	Less than ⅛ teaspoon
60 drops =	1 teaspoon
1 teaspoon =	⅓ tablespoon
1 tablespoon =	3 teaspoons or ½ ounce
2 tablespoons =	1 fluid ounce
4 tablespoons =	¼ cup
5⅓ tablespoons =	⅓ cup
8 tablespoons =	½ cup or 4 ounces
16 tablespoons =	1 cup or 8 ounces
1 cup =	½ pint or 8 fluid ounces
2 cups =	1 pint
4 cups =	32 ounces or 1 quart
1 pint liquid =	16 ounces
1 quart liquid =	2 pints or 32 ounces
1 gallon liquid =	4 quarts
⅕ gallon or ⅘ quart =	25.6 ounces

U.S. Dry Measure Equivalents

Dry measure pints and quarts are about one-sixteenth larger than liquid measure pints and quarts. Dry measure is used for large quantities of raw fruits.

1 quart = 2 pints
8 quarts = 1 peck
4 pecks = 1 bushel

Weight Or Avoirdupois Equivalents

1 ounce = 16 drams
1 pound = 16 ounces
1 kilo = 2.20 pounds

U.S. and British Measure Equivalents

Although many British units of measurement have the same name as those in the United States, they are not all identical. Generally weights are equivalent, but volumes are not.

U.S.
The standard measuring cup or U.S. gill is:
8 ounces = 16 tablespoons = 48 teaspoons

British
The standard measuring cup or Imperial gill is:
10 oz. = 20 U.S. tablespoons = 60 U.S. teaspoons

Liquid Measure Volume Equivalents

1¼ U.S. teaspoons =	1 English *tea*spoon
1¼ U.S. tablespoon =	1 English *table*spoon
1 U.S. gill =	⅚ English *tea*cup
2 U.S. gills =	⅚ English *breakfast* cup
1 U.S. cup =	⅚ English *breakfast* cup
1 U.S. gill =	⅚ English *Imperial* gill
1. U.S. pint =	⅚ English *Imperial* pint
1 U.S. quart =	⅚ English *Imperial* quart
1 U.S. gallon =	⅚ English *Imperial* gallon

U.S. Liquid and Volume Measures and Metric Equivalents

1 teaspoon =	5 milliliters
1 tablespoon =	15 milliliters
1 ounce =	29.5 milliliters
1 cup (8 ounces) =	237 milliliters
1 pint (16 ounces) =	473 milliliters
⅕ gallon or "fifth" =	¾ liter
1 quart =	.946 liter
½ gallon =	1.9 liters
1 gallon =	3.78 liters

U.S. Weight Measures and Metric Equivalents

1 ounce (avoirdupois) =	28.35 grams
¼ pound =	113.4 grams
½ pound =	226.8 grams
1 pound =	454 grams
5 pounds =	2.27 kilograms

TRADEMARKS

The following are registered trademarks:

American Creme
Arrow
Baileys Original Irish Cream
Benedictine
Carolans
Conticream
Cremaretto
Emmets
Häagen-Dazs
Kalùa
Leroux
Midori
Myers's Original Rum Cream
Original Cream
O'Darby
Tia Maria
Venetian Cream
Waterford Cream
Wimbledon
VOV

Bibliography

Cream liqueurs are so new that there are no books that provide background information on the subject. Even food technology books do not contain information on the subject. The books listed below do provide baking and liqueur-making basics. Literally thousands of cookbooks have recipes to which cream liqueurs may be added successfully.

Burgess, Jillian. *The Coffee Book.* London: Kato Press Unlimited, 1984.

Chanin, Myra. *Mother Wonderful's Cheesecakes and Other Goodies.* New York: Bantam Books, 1982.

McGee, Harold. *On Food and Cooking.* New York: Charles Scribner's Sons, 1984.

Meilach, Dona and Mel. *Homemade Liqueurs.* Chicago: Contemporary Books, Inc., 1979.

Meilach, Dona Z. *Marinade Magic.* Chicago: Contemporary Books, Inc., 1981.

Montagne, Prosper. *The New Larousse Gastronomique.* New York: Crown Publishers, Inc., 1977.

Rombauer, Irma S., and Becker, Marion Rombauer. *The Joy of Cooking.* New York: New American Library, 1974.

Sennett, Bob (Ed). *The Complete World Bartender Guide.* New York: Baronet Publishing Co., 1977.

Index